YOU CAN DO IT!

GRAMMAR

Andy Seed and Roger Hurn

Many thanks to Barbara Seed for acting as consultant on this book

First published in Great Britain in 2011 by Hodder Children's Books

1

A Catalogue record for this book is available from the British Library

ISBN 978 0 340 931219

Book design by Fiona Webb

Project editors: Margaret Conroy and Polly Goodman

Printed and bound by CPI Bookmarque Ltd, Croydon, Surrey

The paper and board used in this paperback by Hodder Children's Books are natural recyclable products made from wood grown in sustainable forests. The manufacturing processes conform to the environmental regulations of the country of origin.

Hodder Children's Books
A division of Hachette Children's Books
338 Euston Road, London NW1 3BH
An Hachette UK Company
www.hachette.co.uk

YOU CAN DO IT!
GRAMMAR

Contents

Meet the Odd Mob

The Odd Mob is a gang of seven friends – a right rabble of different characters, some cool, some clever and some clots. A quick 'who's who' will tell you what you need to know.

Lowdown: questions spin round her head like socks in a tumble dryer.
Likes: question marks
Dislikes: all other punctuation
School report: she loves asking questions – it's a pity she's hopeless at answers.

HMD

Lowdown: this heavy metal dude is the Mob's seriously hairy 70s rocker.
Likes: carrying a guitar at all times, even in the shower.
Dislikes: peace and quiet
School report: a bright pupil whose classic wide-legged stance has greatly improved this year.

Max

Lowdown: Max Mullet is tough, keen and adventurous. Oh, and she's magnetically attracted to trouble.
Likes: having the worst hair in the solar system.
Dislikes: being poked in the eye, liver and fashion
School report: Maxine is very popular, especially with headlice.

Ulf

Lowdown: half-boy half-beast, Ulf is not only as daft as a brush but looks like one.
Likes: grunting, and doing anything which is a naughty no-no.
Dislikes: soap and ballet
School report: shouldn't he be in the zoo?

Flash

Lowdown: the fastest girl on the planet, always in a hurry.
Likes: trackies, trainers and treadmills
Dislikes: waiting
School report: English 14%; Maths 9%; Science 11%; PE 253%

Googal

Lowdown: she's so bright her teachers have to wear sunglasses.
Likes: complicated sums
Dislikes: easy listening
School report: if she was any sharper we could use her to cut cheese.

Deej

Lowdown: so cool he makes cucumbers jealous.
Likes: drum 'n' bass
Dislikes: triangles
School report: the brightest thing about him is the bling he wears.

Shagpile

Lowdown: a carpet, with a tail at one end and a cold wet nose at the other.
Likes: bones, bottoms, lamp-posts
Dislikes: cats, postmen, vets
School report: Tail wagging: great; Barking: loud; Biting: useless; Hungry: always

Mr Sumo

Lowdown: a rude wrestler and big bully who is the gang's evil enemy.
Likes: sitting on people
Dislikes: children, old ladies, baby animals and being fair
School report: expelled for eating the photocopier.
(Not one of the gang.)

You'll also meet two of the Mob's mates, Cheesy Chad and Multiple Joyce, from time to time – they're fun and full of top tips too.

What's It All About?

A quick quiz:

A) Do you enjoy reading grammar books at school? YES/NO
B) Do you read them when you don't have to? YES/NO
C) Do you only bother with grammar when you have to pass a SATs test? YES/NO
D) Do you think grammar's really boring? YES/NO

If you answered NO for questions A and B and YES to questions C and D then CONGRATULATIONS, you're a normal kid!

And you're smart. You learned how to speak English. And did you need a teacher to help you figure out how to do it? No, you didn't. You learnt it when you were a baby – which is pretty amazing. OK. You're great at learning stuff so why do you need this book? Here's the answer. You're already smart but this book can make you smarter at grammar. It's like having an extra brain you can keep in your pocket – only not so squelchy. And you don't have to go to school to read it either.

Questions you won't find answers to in this book

Do cows have calf muscles?
Why isn't there mouse-flavoured cat food?
What does cheese say when it has its photo taken?

So what IS in this book?

Help to avoid embarrassing situations like this.

Teacher: *Are you good at grammar?*
You: *Yes and no.*
Teacher: *What do you mean, 'Yes' and 'No'?*
You: *Yes, I'm no good at grammar.*

So, as Cheesy Chad says …

If you want to find out more about grammar – read this book.
If you want to meet the Odd Mob – read this book.
If you want to impress your friends with a load of jokes – read this book.
If you're shipwrecked on a desert island and are starving hungry – eat this book.

If you also need help with punctuation and spelling, there are two more Odd Mob books to sort you out. Remember, You Can Do It!

How the pages work

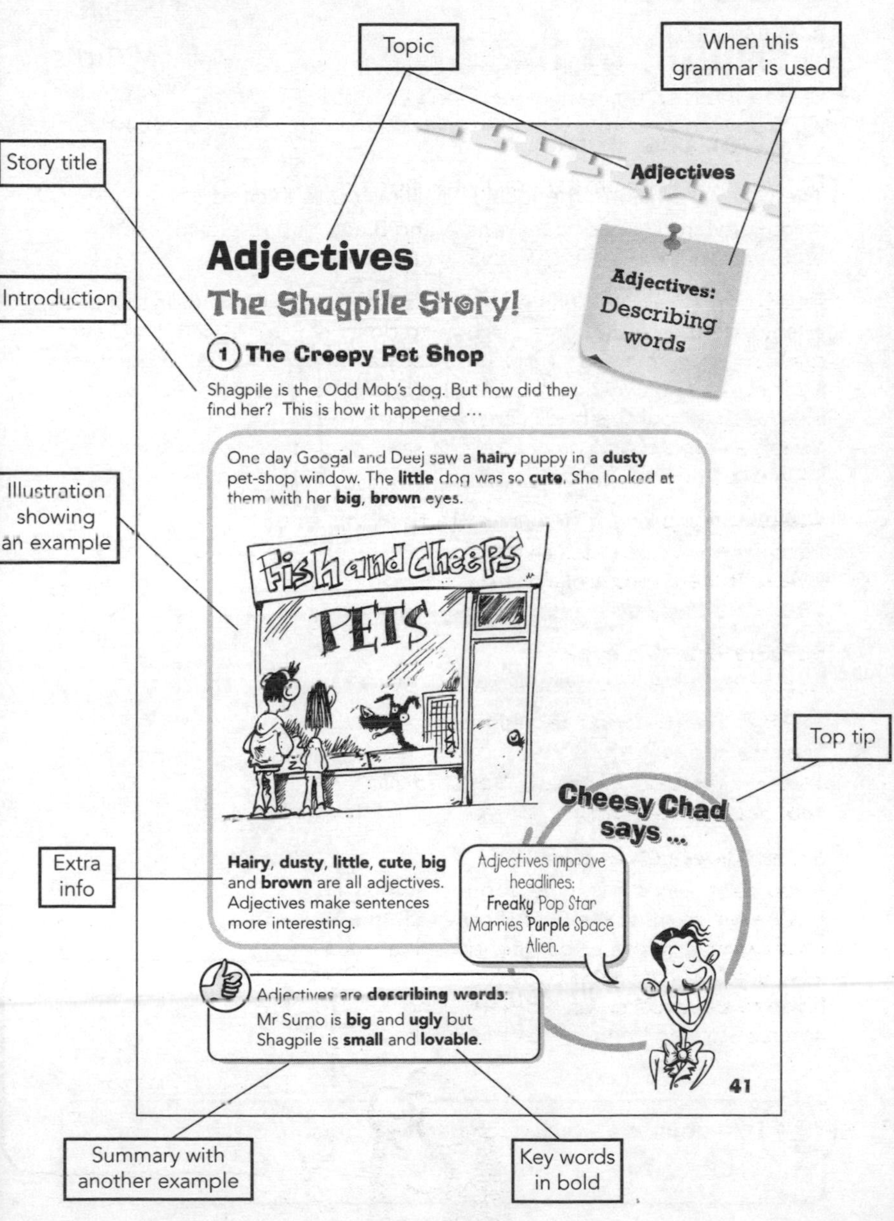

Topic
When this grammar is used
Story title
Introduction
Illustration showing an example
Extra info
Top tip
Summary with another example
Key words in bold
Adjectives
Adjectives
The Shagpile Story!
1 The Creepy Pet Shop
Shagpile is the Odd Mob's dog. But how did they find her? This is how it happened …
Adjectives: Describing words
One day Googal and Deej saw a **hairy** puppy in a **dusty** pet-shop window. The **little** dog was so **cute**. She looked at them with her **big**, **brown** eyes.
Fish and Cheeps
PETS
Hairy, **dusty**, **little**, **cute**, **big** and **brown** are all adjectives. Adjectives make sentences more interesting.
Cheesy Chad says …
Adjectives improve headlines: **Freaky** Pop Star Marries **Purple** Space Alien.
Adjectives are **describing words**.
Mr Sumo is **big** and **ugly** but Shagpile is **small** and **lovable**.
41

Nouns

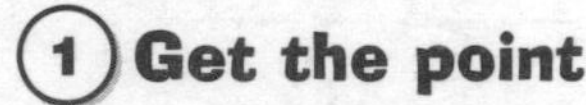

Nouns:
Naming words

1 Get the point

The gang are visiting the local zoo. Ulf is quite excited …

Zoo

Lion

A **noun** is a word which **names** a person, place or thing:

Ulf zoo parrot mess

Joke Break

Chloe: What do you do if you find a python in your toilet?

Joe: Wait till he's finished.

2 The bear facts

Max and Deej are reading about the local zoo's new arrival.

Proper nouns: Names that need a capital letter

This giant panda has just arrived at Bigmouth Zoo from China. His name is Choo-Choo. We're training him. He will be 5 years old in April.

Look at those eyes – just got here and he's been in a fight already.

Why do some of these words have capital letters?

They're proper nouns – names of particular people, places and things.

A **proper noun** is the name of an **individual** person, place or thing:

Bigmouth Zoo   China   Choo-Choo   April

Common nouns:
Name a type of thing

3 Crocodile rock

Flash and HMD somehow take the wrong turning at the zoo …

What are we going to do? We need to frighten them away somehow.

There are lots of **common nouns** causing bother here: snakes, baboons, tigers, crocodiles, rockers …

A **common noun** is a **kind of** person, place or thing:

zoo   ape   guitar   boy

4 Never herd the question

Wozza joins the gang at the zoo. As usual, she is full of questions …

Collective nouns: Groups of things

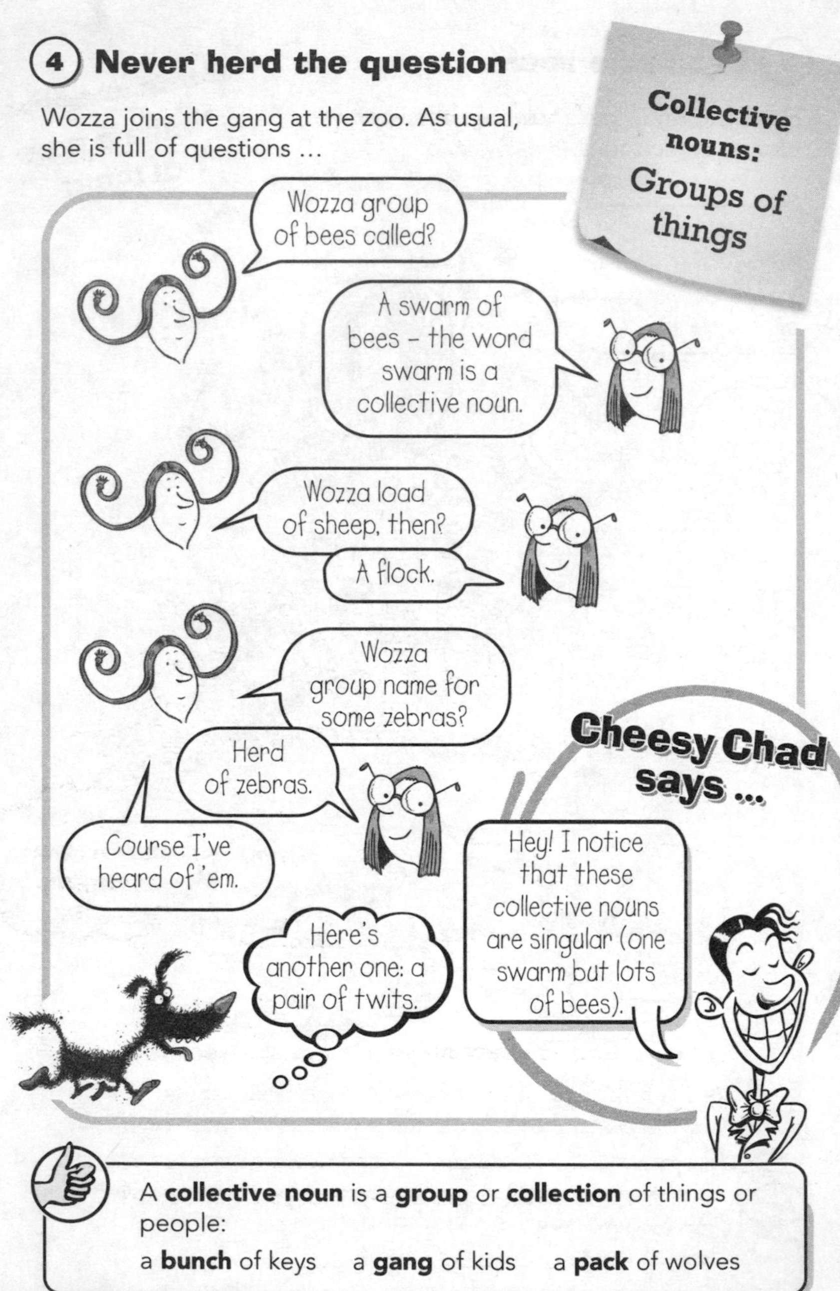

Wozza group of bees called?
A swarm of bees – the word swarm is a collective noun.
Wozza load of sheep, then?
A flock.
Wozza group name for some zebras?
Herd of zebras.
Course I've heard of 'em.
Here's another one: a pair of twits.
Cheesy Chad says ...
Hey! I notice that these collective nouns are singular (one swarm but lots of bees).

A **collective noun** is a **group** or **collection** of things or people:

a **bunch** of keys a **gang** of kids a **pack** of wolves

Abstract nouns: Things you can't touch

5 Panda wonder

Oh dear, Choo-Choo the panda has escaped from his cage at the zoo.

It's a **mystery**.

I suppose he wanted his **freedom**.

Pandas have so much **strength**.

What's the **excitement** about?

I heard a **noise**.

I feel just a touch of **fear**.

Shall I show them **kindness** or **cruelty**? Hee hee.

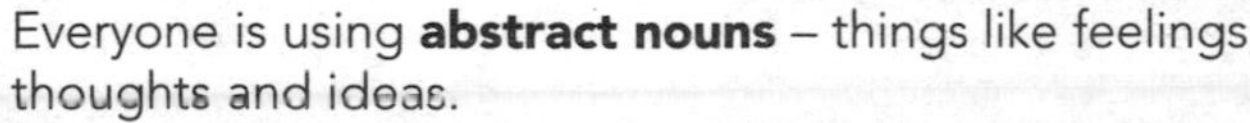

Everyone is using **abstract nouns** – things like feelings, thoughts and ideas.

An **abstract noun** is something that **you can't touch or see**:

power love silence sleep

6 A quick round-up

A test for nouns: Using 'the'

They've found the panda and he turns out to be friendly after all. They find a load of other escaped animals too.

I'm glad this is the end of our zoo adventure.

Yes, it's been fun, despite the pain and terror.

The cheek! Actually, there are two cheeks...

Good job we solved the problem earlier – it's dark now.

Multiple Joyce

Which of these is correct?

A A pant of ants.
B A gerroff of ants.
C An army of ants.
D Afraid of ants.

You can test if a word is a noun by putting '**the**' in front of it. If it makes sense, the word is a noun.

Nouns make sense with the word 'the' in front of them:

the end ✓ **the pain** ✓ **the cheek** ✓ **the disaster** ✓

the glad ✗ the in ✗ the despite ✗ the went ✗

Plurals

Odd Mob Hobbies

Plurals:
Plural means more than one

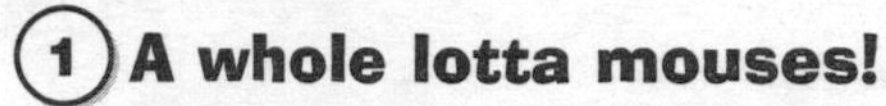

1 A whole lotta mouses!

Max is writing an email to her pen friend in Mongolia.

My hobby is looking after my pets. I have 3 dogs, 4 cats, 2 hamsters and 486 <u>mouses</u>.

The spell check has spotted that '*mouses*' isn't right, Max. The plural of *mouse* is *mice*. Plural just means *more than one*.

Whoopsidoodle!

Singular means **one** and **plural** means **two or more**:

<u>Singular</u>	<u>Plural</u>
cat	cats
hobby	hobbies

2 Rock and run

Let's find out about the rest of the gang's hobbies …

Plurals:
Add 's' to most nouns

HMD loves to play the **guitar**. He has five **guitars** altogether.

Flash loves a **race**. She has won over 967 **races**.

Most **plurals** of **nouns** are formed by adding **s**:

guitar → guitar**s** word → word**s**

race → race**s** achievement → achievement**s**

Plurals:
Notice plural endings

③ Question time

What are Googal's and Wozza's hobbies, I wonder?

Googal is usually at a **quiz**. She loves going to **quizzes**.

Wozza is a **shelf** expert. She doesn't always get her **shelves** level though.

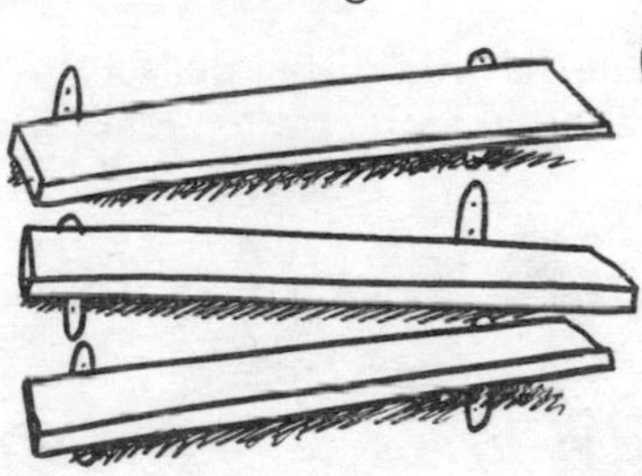

There are lots of other plural endings to spot – check them out in the Odd Mob book *You Can Do It: Spelling*.

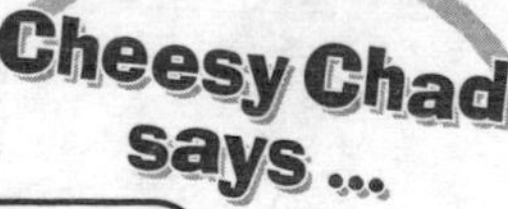

Add **es** to nouns ending in **o** to make the plural.

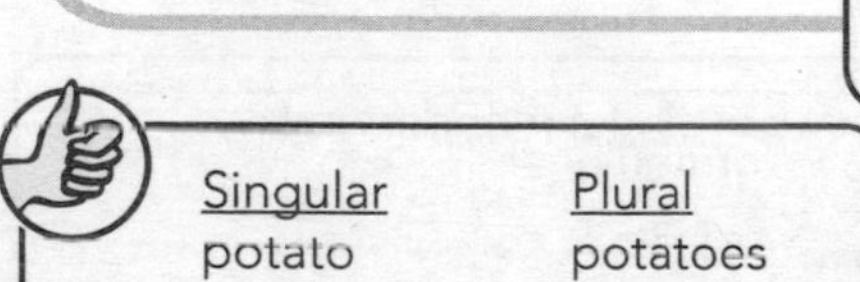

Singular	Plural
potato	potatoes
wolf	wolves

4 Fish and sheeps

Do Deej and Ulf have hobbies too?
Of course they do!

Plurals:
Can be the same as the singular

Deej is a tropical **fish** fancier. He has two cool **fish** in his aquarium.

Ulf has a **sheep** hairball collection. He has 67 hairballs from **sheep** at home. The less said about that the better, really.

Oh deer

Some nouns are the same in singular and plural:

One **sheep**, two **sheep**
One **moose**, two **moose**
One **deer**, 500 **deer**

Plurals:
Irregular plurals

 Mmm ... sweet

Mr Sumo and Shagpile also each have a hobby.

Mr Sumo is a **person** who just loves wrestling. He can wrestle four **people** at once.

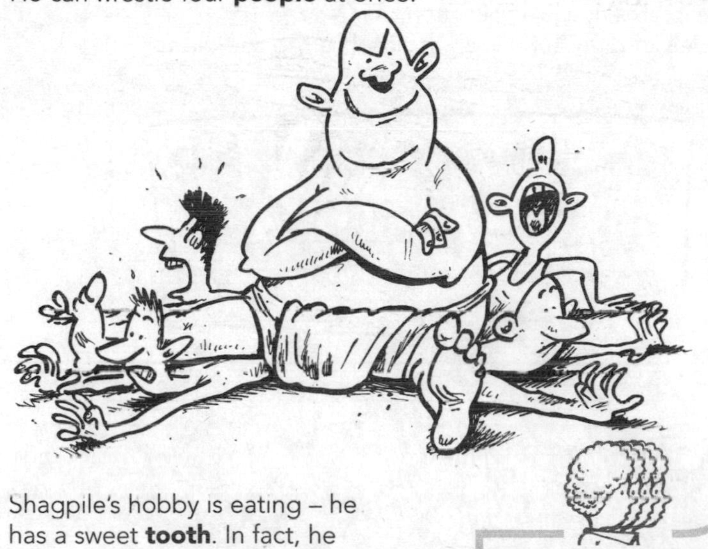

Shagpile's hobby is eating – he has a sweet **tooth**. In fact, he has lots of sweet **teeth**.

Multiple Joyce

Which of these plurals is correct?

A bacteriums
B bacterii
C bacteria
D 'orrible germs

The words **people** and **teeth** are examples of **irregular plurals**. Here are some more:

man – men child – children cactus – cacti
foot – feet medium – media louse – lice

Pronouns

Scary Monsters

Pronouns:
Take the place of nouns

1 Dinosaur park

The local park has a collection of life-sized models of dinosaurs. The Odd Mob go to see them.

This way to the Dinosaurs
She's right but I'm still not going to get too close.
I can't wait to see them.
They'll be really scary.
They don't scare me. I can outrun them.
Flash – they're only models.
Cheesy Chad says ...
A noun is a word that names something and a pronoun is a word that can be used in place of a noun.

A **pronoun** can be used instead of the name of a person or a thing:

He (Ulf) wanted to see **them** (the model dinosaurs).

② It's getting personal

The Odd Mob can't agree on which dinosaurs to go and see first.

Pronouns:
Personal pronouns – used instead of names

I'm going to see the Tyrannosaurus. Who's coming with **me**?
Max, Googal and **I** want to see the Diplodocus. Why don't **you** come with **us**?

You don't want to go with **them**.

You want to come with **us**. **They** won't have fun but **we** will. **We**'re going to climb on the Stegosaurus.

Using **personal pronouns** like **I**, **me**, **we**, **us**, **you**, **they**, **them** helps improve your writing by making it less repetitive.

Joke Break

Q: What do you give a dinosaur when it's feeling sick?

A: Lots of room.

Use **personal pronouns** instead of repeating the name of someone or something:

Shagpile hopes the dinosaur isn't going to eat <u>Shagpile</u>. ✗
Shagpile hopes the dinosaur isn't going to eat <u>**her**</u>. ✓

③ Who'd be a dentist?

Pronouns:
Demonstrative pronouns

In the end the Odd Mob decide to stick together.

Hey, look at **that**.
No, look at **this**.
These dinosaurs are really cool.
Wow, have you seen the size of **those** teeth?
I'd hate to be **that** Tyrannosaurus's dentist.

The **demonstrative pronouns** are: **this**, **that**, **these** and **those**.

Demonstrative pronouns stand in for a person, place or thing that must be pointed to:

Those who want to see the dinosaur models must wait for the park to open.

Pronouns: Indefinite pronouns

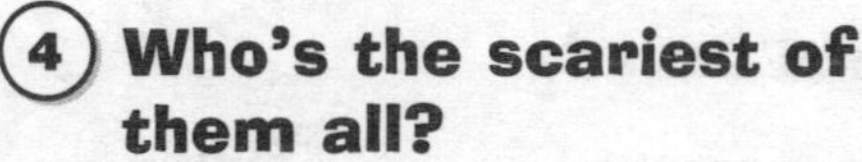

4 Who's the scariest of them all?

The Odd Mob try to decide which of the dinosaurs they would least like to meet on a dark night.

Some of these dinosaurs are scarier than others.

I don't care what **anyone** says, that Tyrannosaurus is the scariest.

Many people would agree with you, Deej.

Nobody in their right mind's going to diss a Tyrannosaurus.

Wait a minute, I thought I heard **something**.

It can't have been the dinosaurs. **None** of them is alive.

But do **any** of the dinosaurs know that?

Indefinite pronouns give the idea of **all**, **any**, **none**, or **some** but they don't refer to actual people, places or things:

Something is going on here but **nobody** knows what it is.

5 King of the terrible lizards

Pronouns: Interrogative pronouns

The Odd Mob get a nasty shock when the Tyrannosaurus Rex roars at them.

ROAR!

What was that noise?

It's one of the dinosaurs but **which** one?

It's the T Rex!

Whose daft idea was it to come here?

Who cares? Let's run!

To **whom** can the Odd Mob turn for help?
Find out on the next page …

There are five **interrogative pronouns**: what, which, who, whom, and whose.

Interrogative pronouns are used to ask questions:
Who was that? **What** was that? **Which** one was that?

6 A mystery explained

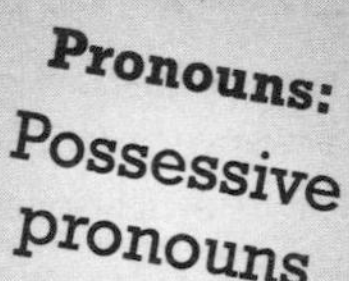

The Odd Mob run headlong into the park keeper and tell him their terrifying tale.

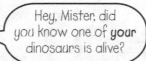

Hey, Mister, did you know one of **your** dinosaurs is alive?

Yeah, it nearly scared us out of **our** wits when we heard **its** roar.

The dinosaurs aren't **mine**. But you kids must be out of **your** minds if you think they're real.

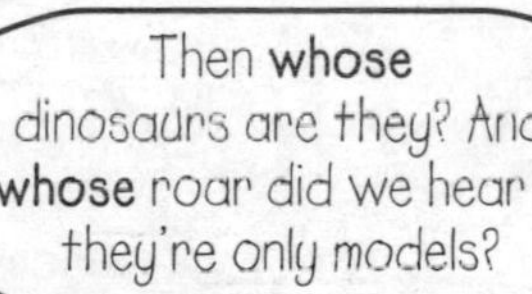

Then **whose** dinosaurs are they? And **whose** roar did we hear if they're only models?

The dinosaur models are owned by Mr Sumo. The Tyrannosaurus has a secret trapdoor in **its** back and it's **his** idea of a joke to hide inside it and roar at people.

Grrr. We'll get **our** own back on him.

Possessive pronouns show whose something is:

Max's heart was in **her** mouth when the dinosaur roared **its** terrible roar.

7 The tables are turned

Pronouns: Relative pronouns

The person who's been hired to promote the dinosaur exhibition has gone off to lunch and left their dinosaur costume behind.

Hmm. This dinosaur costume **which** someone's left here has given me an idea.

This costume is going to give Mr Sumo a fright **whichever** way he looks at it.

Help! I'll pay a monster reward to **whoever** saves me from this monster.

Joke Break

Q: What do you get if you cross a dinosaur with a pig?

A: Jurassic Pork!

The **relative pronouns** are: as, who, whom, that, which, whoever, whomever, whatever, whose, what and whichever.

Relative pronouns join different parts of a sentence together:

The person **who** laughs last, laughs longest.

Pronouns: Reflexive pronouns

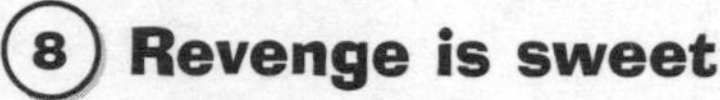

8 Revenge is sweet

Mr Sumo has ended up in the boating lake. It's too bad he didn't take a boat.

The Odd Mob are laughing **themselves** silly at the sight of Mr Sumo sitting in the boating lake. He jumped in to save **himself** from the dinosaur.

We fooled Mr Sumo. He thought it was a real dinosaur chasing him but it was only **ourselves** inside that costume!

Joke Break

Q: What do you call a dinosaur that sleeps all day?

A: A dino-snore!

Reflexive pronouns sound a bit selfish because they always end in 'self' or 'selves':

Yourself, **myself**, **herself**, **himself**, **itself**, **ourselves**, **yourselves**, **themselves**.

Reflexive pronouns always refer to another noun or **pronoun** in the sentence:

Mr Sumo had no one to blame but **himself**.

Pronouns: Examples

9 Wozza's book about dinosaurs

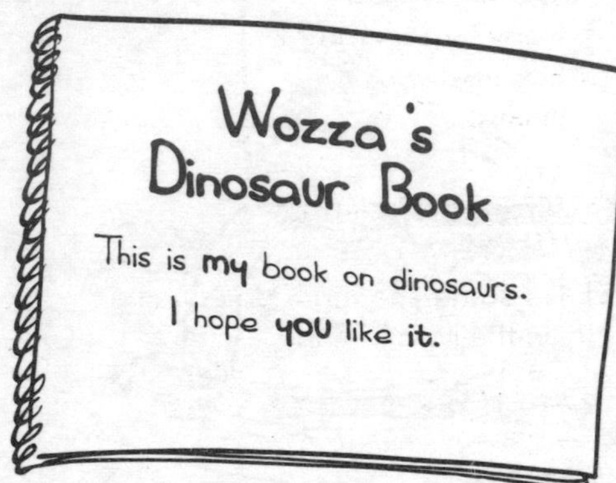

Wozza's used three nouns (Wozza, Dinosaur, Book) and four **personal pronouns** in her introduction. **Pronouns** take the place of nouns. **Personal pronouns** save you repeating names.

Demonstrative pronouns like **these**, **they**, **that** and **those** point out something or someone.

Pronouns: Examples

Some dinosaurs
were meat-eaters
but most ate
plants.

Indefinite pronouns like **some** and **most** don't name things directly. They give the idea of things in general.

Dinosaurs were reptiles
which meant they laid
eggs. Though, once
hatched, baby
dinosaurs had to
fend for
themselves.

Relative pronouns like **which** link different parts of a sentence together while a **reflexive pronoun** like **themselves** links to another noun or **pronoun** in the sentence.

Wozza's Dinosaur Quiz

1) **Which** dinosaur was called 'The King'?
2) **What** did the Brontosaurus eat?
3) **Who** would win in a fight between T Rex and Mr Sumo?

Wozza has used **interrogative pronouns** to ask questions in her quiz.

Multiple Joyce

Which of these is a pronoun?

A protein
B proboscis
C pro-am
D her

Verbs

Sports Day

Verbs:
Action words

1 Winner takes all

It's Sports Day at the Odd Mob's school.

Flash **sprints** faster than a bullet.

Flash **hops** further than a kangaroo.

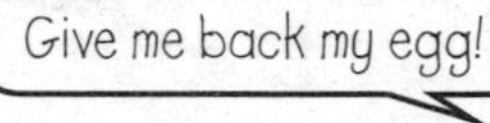

Flash won the egg and spoon race – but only just!

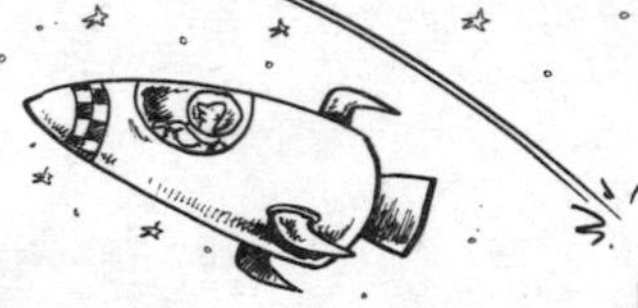

Flash **throws** the javelin higher than a space rocket.

Cheesy Chad says ...

Any word that works when you put 'to' in front of it is a verb. For example, **to walk**, **to swim**, **to laugh** are verbs but **to hippopotamus** isn't.

A verb is usually an **action** word:

leap run jump think

2 The human trampoline

Verbs:
State of being verbs

After winning the high jump, Flash is looking for new challenges.

Flash **is** going for a new record in the high jump. But what **are** her chances? Can she really leap over Mr Sumo or **is** she **being** silly?
She'll **be** bounced into the middle of next week if she lands on his tummy!

Flash decides a human like Mr Sumo wouldn't want to **be** used as a trampoline, so she passes on her attempt to jump over him.

Here are some examples of state of being verbs:

is, **am**, **were**, **was**, **are**, **be**, **being**, **been**.

State of being verbs tell you that something **IS**. They can be the main **verb** of the sentence:

Shagpile **is** the Odd Mob's dog.

3 I have a dream

Verbs: Tenses

Oh dear, it looks like Flash has worn herself out.

The **tense** of a verb tells you **when** the action happened. It could be in the past, the present or the future:

Flash **jumps** higher than a mountain. (Present)

Yesterday Flash **ran** faster than a train. (Past)

Tomorrow Flash **will win** the cup. (Future)

Well, she does in her dreams.

Googal, you're for the high jump today.
Why? I haven't done anything wrong.

Joke Break

Q: What do runners do when they forget something?

A: They jog their memory.

Verbs can be in three main **tenses** – the past, the present and the future:

THE PAST	THE PRESENT
Flash trained hard	Flash is training hard

THE FUTURE

Flash will train hard

Verbs: Auxiliary verbs

4 It takes two

Ulf and HMD decide to take part in the three-legged race.

Doh! I told you we only **had** to tie *two* of our legs together!
Sorry. But I'm no good at counting.

Verbs sometimes use an extra word called an **auxiliary** verb to help them:

If you tie your legs together and run, you **might** fall over too.

Joke Break

Q: Why should you never have a race with a big cat?

A: Because it might be a cheetah.

The most common auxiliary verbs are: **be**, **do**, **have**, **can**, **could**, **will**, **would**, **should**, **may**, **might**, **must**.

Auxiliary verbs help the main verb in a sentence:

Mr Sumo **could** win the egg and spoon race (but he **will** have to glue the egg to the spoon first).

5 Under the hammer

Verbs: Active verbs

Mr Sumo decides to show the Odd Mob he is a star athlete too.

Mr Sumo **throws** the hammer.

The hammer **flies** through the air.

It **smashes** a window.

The angry home owner **hurls** the hammer back to Mr Sumo.

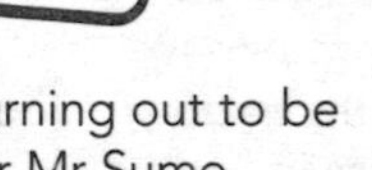

This Sports Day is turning out to be quite a headache for Mr Sumo ...

Cheesy Chad says ...

Remember, active verbs are more powerful than passive verbs. They are 'tough guy' verbs.

Active verbs show who or what carried out an action:

The hammer **hit** Mr Sumo on his head.

6 The glittering prizes

Googal has written a report of the Sports Day for the school magazine.

Verbs: Passive verbs

Our School Sports Day
by Googal

Sports Day wasn't much fun at first as all the races ***were won*** *by Flash. But then it* ***was decided*** *that she couldn't enter the three-legged race because she's only got two legs!*

The highlight of the day was when Mr Sumo ***was hit*** *on the head by a hammer. This* ***was enjoyed*** *by everyone – except Mr Sumo. But he cheered up when the first prize in the 'Biggest bump on your bonce' competition* ***was won*** *by him.*

They might be shy and quiet but you don't need a telescope to spot passive verbs. They often have helping verbs (**is**, **am**, **are**, **were**, **was**, **been**) in front of them, or the word 'by' after them.

Multiple Joyce

Which of these is a verb?

A Superman
B Batman
C He-Man
D Limp

Look for the person/thing the sentence is about.
If an action is done **to** it/him/her, then the verb is **passive**:
Mr Sumo **was bitten** by Shagpile.

Tenses

Sticky situations

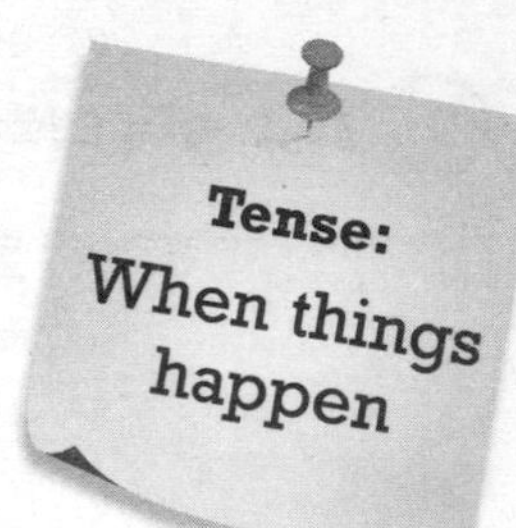

1 Yesterday, today and tomorrow

Ulf is in the sweet shop, deciding what to buy.

Yesterday I **bought** a lot of toffee. It **was** yummy, but I **felt** quite sick afterwards.

Ulf is talking about the **past**.

TOFFEE

Tomorrow, I **will buy** lots more toffee. I **will feel** quite sick after that too, I should think ...

Ulf is talking about the **future**.

Today, I **am buying** some bubble gum – I **feel** that my stomach needs a rest!

Ulf is talking about the **present**.

The **tense** of a sentence tells you **when** things happen.
Past tense: what has happened
Present tense: what is happening
Future tense: what will happen

2 Today's the day!

Ulf meets Flash outside the sweet shop.

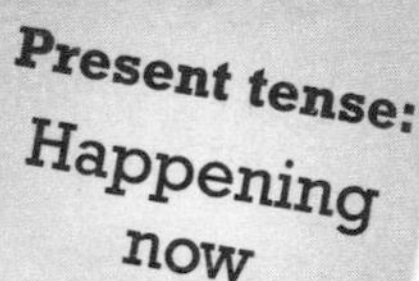

Present tense:
Happening now

Blow, Ulf! Blow now!
I am blowing!

Blow harder, Ulf. Come on, BLOW!

Oh, blow!

The **present tense** is all about what happens **now**.

I **eat**	we **are eating**
he **chews**	they are **chewing**

3 It's all in the past

Ulf and Flash need help ...

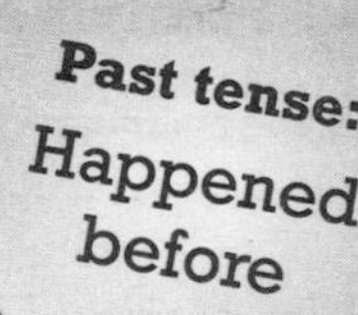

Past tense:
Happened before

What happened to you, Ulf?

Well, I **was blowing** a mega bubble. Flash **told** me to blow harder, so I **blew** and I **blew**.

Yeah, it **was** great! He **was blowing** so hard, that he **blew** a hole in it, and it splatter**ed** all over his face.

Oh dear, you really **have blown** it this time, Ulf!

Cheesy Chad says ...

You can make the past tense by adding '**ed**' to many verbs, like chew**ed**, want**ed** and scratch**ed**.

You can change or add to the **verb** to make the **past tense**:

buy – **bought** catch – **caught**

eat – **was eating**

4 Future plans

Thank goodness – Googal's arrived. She'll be able to help poor Ulf.

Future tense: Hasn't happened yet

Will you **help** me?
I'm a bit stuck ...

We **are going to put** you under a shower. It **might be** a bit cold, but you **will look** better later.

I **am going to blow-dry** my hair now.

The **future tense** tells you what **will** or **might** happen:

I **am going** to cry

You **will** not **laugh** at me

We **might help** you

5 Tenses don't mix!

Tenses:
Don't mix your tenses

Flash tells the story of Ulf's disaster in an email to Deej.

Oh dear – poor Flash has got her tenses all mixed up. Can you spot where she went wrong?

New Message

Hi Deej,

It was so funny – you should see it! Ulf has this bubble gum, and I say 'Blow!' So he will blow and blow, and the bubble pop. The gum went right over his face and is all in his hair. Googal will tell him he needed a shower. It take ages for him to clean himself up! Ulf did not do that again in the future, I can tell you.

Flash

Hey, Flash, you're looking a bit tense! Shall I help you put this right?

New Message

Hi Deej,

It was so funny – you should have seen it! Ulf had this bubble gum, and I said 'Blow!' So he blew and blew, and the bubble popped. The gum went right over his face and was all in his hair. Googal told him he needed a shower. It took ages for him to clean himself up! Ulf will not do that again in the future, I can tell you.

Flash

Multiple Joyce

Which of these is in the past tense?

A I will explode
B I am exploding
C I exploded
D Boom!

Mixing up your **tenses** can make your writing confusing to read.

Adjectives

The Shagpile Story!

Adjectives: Describing words

1 The Creepy Pet Shop

Shagpile is the Odd Mob's dog. But how did they find her? This is how it happened …

One day Googal and Deej saw a **hairy** puppy in a **dusty** pet-shop window. The **little** dog was so **cute**. She looked at them with her **big**, **brown** eyes.

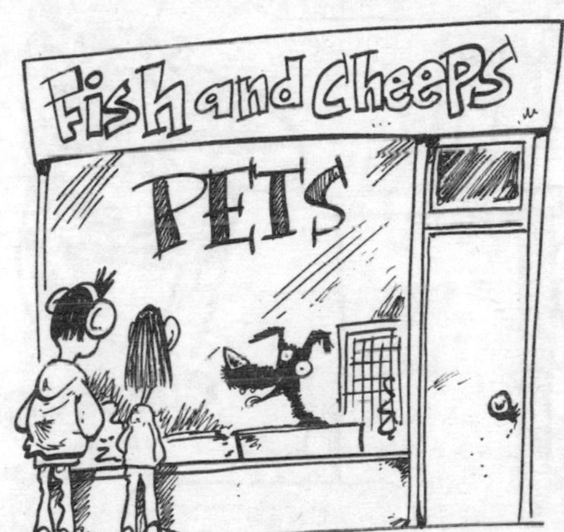

Hairy, **dusty**, **little**, **cute**, **big** and **brown** are all adjectives. Adjectives make sentences more interesting.

Cheesy Chad says …

Adjectives improve headlines: **Freaky** Pop Star Marries **Purple** Space Alien.

Adjectives are **describing words**: Mr Sumo is **big** and **ugly** but Shagpile is **small** and **lovable**.

2 The little shop of horrors

Googal and Deej just had to buy the lovable little puppy so they went into the creepy old shop.

Adjectives: Describe people, places and things
Excuse me, **scary** shopkeeper, but is that **adorable**, **bouncy** bundle of **playful** puppy for sale?
Do you mean that **mangy** mongrel with the **cold**, **wet** nose who's putting her **muddy** paws all over my **clean** window?
Cheesy Chad says ...
Never put an adjective after a noun: It's a fierce dog NOT a dog fierce.

Gosh, from the way he's described her it doesn't seem as if the pet shop man liked the puppy very much. Let's hope he agreed to sell her to Googal and Deej.

Adjectives tell you more about nouns (naming words). They usually come before the noun:

scary shopkeeper   **playful** puppy   **mangy** mongrel

3 A dog's for life

Deej was worried that the shopkeeper didn't seem to like animals.

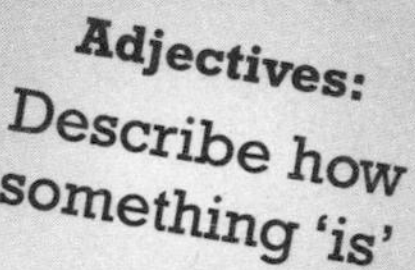

Adjectives:
Describe how something 'is'

Hey, mister, aren't pet shop owners supposed to be **kind**, **gentle** and **friendly** to the pets?

Yes, but I find pets are **bothersome** beasts. They're too **noisy** and **smelly** for me. When I've sold this **last**, **lonely** **little** mutt I'm going to open a **terrific** taxidermist's shop.

Hmm ... it looks like Googal and Deej arrived just in time to save the puppy from a **fearsome** fate!

Cheesy Chad says ...

Adjectives can give you lots of information about nouns. For example: The prince is **vain**, **silly** and **cruel**.

I wouldn't want him kissing me, then.

You can use more than one adjective to give information about **how something is**:

The shopkeeper had **cold**, **cruel** eyes the colour of **dirty** dishwater.

Adjectives: Possessive adjectives

4 Deal or no deal

Googal and Deej tried to make a deal with the shopkeeper.

Well, do you want to buy **my** dog or not? It's **her** last chance to find a new owner. She could be **your** dog for only £10.
Is that **your** best price? OK then – we'll take **her**. That's all **our** pocket money for the week gone but she's worth it!

Thank goodness Googal and Deej were the puppy's new owners. Who knows what would have happened to her if they hadn't come along?

Joke Break

Q: What type of dog is always getting into fights?

A: A boxer!

Possessive adjectives include: **his**, **her**, **its**, **my**, **our**, **their**, **your**.

Possessive adjectives tell who something belongs to:
It's **my** pocket money. She's **our** dog.

5 A dog by any other name

Adjectives: Demonstrative adjectives

Googal and Deej had to think of a good name for their little dog.

What are we going to call **this** dog, Googal?
That is a question which needs an answer.
These days nobody calls their dog 'Rover' or 'Fido'. **Those** names are so old-fashioned.
Hmm ... she looks like a hairy carpet so we'll call her Shagpile.

It could have been worse – they could have called her Axminster. At least Shagpile seemed to like her new name.

Joke Break

Q: What kind of dog loves having its hair washed?

A: A shampoodle!

The demonstrative adjectives **that**, **these**, **this**, **those** are words that point to a noun:

Shagpile's going to chase **that** cat.

Those sausages look tasty to Shagpile.

Now Shagpile is part of the gang and they think she is fantastic, but Mr Sumo's not so sure.

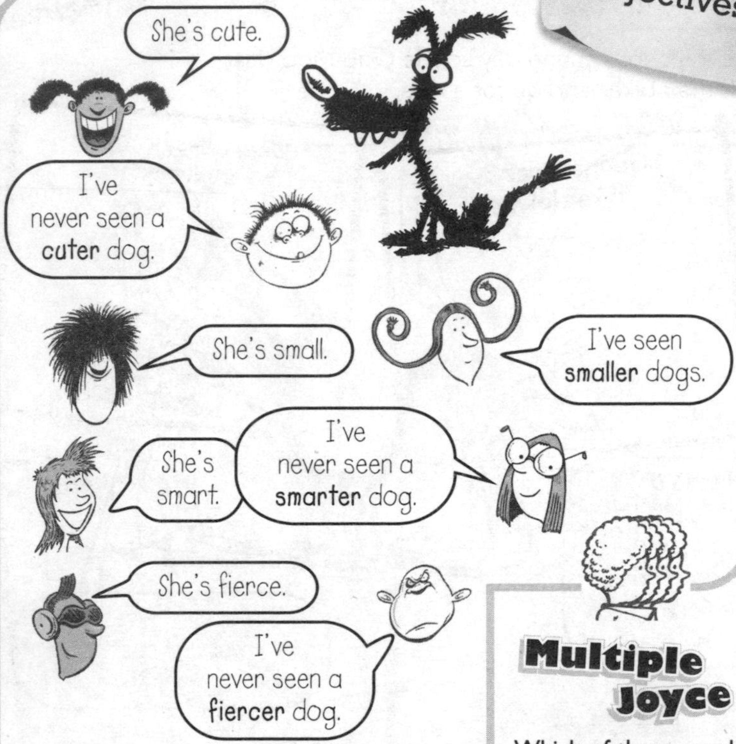

Adjectives: Comparative adjectives

She's cute.

I've never seen a **cuter** dog.

She's small.

I've seen **smaller** dogs.

She's smart.

I've never seen a **smarter** dog.

She's fierce.

I've never seen a **fiercer** dog.

Poor old Mr Sumo. He already has enough trouble trying to get the better of the Odd Mob without having to worry about Shagpile too!

Multiple Joyce

Which of these words is an adjective?

A Verb
B Noun
C Clever
D Adjective

You can use **comparative adjectives** to compare the differences between things:

Mr Roly Poly was **heavy**. Mr Lardy was **heavier**, but Mr Sumo was **heaviest**.

Adverbs

On Your Bike

Adverbs:
Tell us about verbs

1 Tour de Bognor

It's a glorious spring day so the Odd Mob dust off their bikes and go for a ride.

Googal rides her bike **slowly**.

Deej rides his bike **stylishly**.

Flash rides her bike **powerfully**.

Ulf rides his bike **badly**.

The words in bold above tell us **how** the riding is done. Each one is an **adverb**.

Adverbs tell us something about a **verb**.

Adverbs often tell us **how** actions happen:

run **quickly** type **carefully**
sing **well** talk **quietly**

Cheesy Chad says ...

Adverbs can tell us about adjectives too.

2 Gone in 60 minutes

No one can find Flash until Wozza, HMD and Max suddenly bump into her.

Adverbs:
Can tell where action happens

Flash! We've looked **everywhere** for you!
Yeah, we've been searching **here** and **there**, man.
You've been **away** for an hour – where did you go?
Whoops, sorry – I didn't think it would take me that long to cycle **around** Britain ...

Adverbs can tell us **where** actions take place. Each adverb in bold above **describes** where something happened. Can you spot the **verb** in each case?

Joke Break

Q: My silly dog chases anyone on a bike.

A: Well, take away his bike, then.

Adverbs sometimes tell us **where** actions happen:

come **here** walk **there** go **home**
look **away** sit **nearby**

3 Penny fall thing

The gang are just about to set off home when Googal has a little problem with her ancient bike …

Adverbs: Can tell when actions happen

Today is not my lucky day!
Has this happened **before**?
Only 7 or 8 times. I fell off **yesterday** too.

I'll try and fix it **now**.
That's good – I may need the bike **tomorrow**.
Do you **always** brake using this?
No, I **never** use that – I just stick my foot in the spokes.

Adverbs can also tell us **when** actions happen.

The seven adverbs in bold above **describe** when something took place.

Adverbs can tell us about verbs in terms of **when**:

never lie | talk **now** | visit **tomorrow**
always stop | go **immediately**

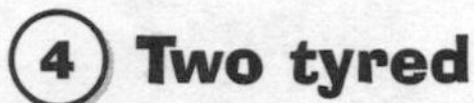

4 Two tyred

After all their bike adventures, the gang are worn out.

Adverbs: Can tell us 'how'

Googal is feeling **very** bruised

Deej is **too** weary to ride.

Ulf is **extremely** tired …
Zzzzz

Even Flash is walking quite **slowly**!

All of these **adverbs** say **how** things were.

Adverbs can tell us about **adjectives** or even **other adverbs**:

too cold
quite badly
very big
really quickly

Cheesy Chad says ...

Try not to overuse adverbs like 'extremely' or 'really' in your writing.

⑤ Top gear?

The next day the gang help Googal choose a new bike ...

Multiple Joyce

Which of these words is an adverb?

A beautiful
B beautifully
C Beautifrilly
D Uglyfully

Most adverbs end in '**ly**', like the ones Googal used above, but not all do. Many common short words, like the gang used, are adverbs too, e.g. **also**, **just**, **less**, **more**, **much**, **even**.

Prepositions

On the river

Prepositions:
Link nouns, pronouns and phrases to other words

1 Mysterious goings on

HMD, Flash and Shagpile are up to something.

Googal hears some hammering coming from **inside** HMD's shed. She peeks **in** to see what is happening.

There are bits **of** wood, nails, wire and string **on** the floor **under** her feet. HMD and Flash stand **before** her holding saws. **Beside** the workbench, Shagpile sits with a hammer **in** her mouth. **Behind** them, Googal can see a weird object leaning **against** the wall.

HMD, Flash and Shagpile have made a raft on oil drums **inside** the shed **without** thinking about how they can get it **outside** the shed. They try to drag it **through** the door but it gets stuck!

The problem is solved when the rest of the Odd Mob come **along** and lift the shed **up** so they can pull **out** the raft.

Joke Break

Q: Where do mice put their boats?

A: In the hickory dickory dock.

Prepositions tell us about the relationship between other words in a sentence:

Shagpile is hiding **behind** the chair.

'**behind**' shows the link between **hiding** and **chair**.

2 An epic journey

The Odd Mob takes the raft to the river to see if it will float.

Prepositions: Usually come before nouns

The Odd Mob carry the raft **over** the stile, **across** the field, **under** the bridge, **along** the muddy path to the river.

Joke Break

Q: Why did the turkey cross the road?

A: To prove he wasn't a chicken.

Prepositions are usually placed before nouns or pronouns:

under the desk
across the sea
over the moon
by the wood

③ Making a splash

Prepositions: Show direction

The gang finally makes it to the river with their raft.

When the Odd Mob get **to** the river they drop the raft **into** the water. Shagpile is so excited. She bounds **along** the riverbank and skids on the mud. She can't stop in time and tumbles **down** into the water.

The Odd Mob race **across** to the water's edge and stare **down** at the terrified Shagpile. Flash jumps **into** the river and rescues her. Luckily, the water only comes **up** to Flash's knees.

'To' is the main **preposition** of direction:

The Odd Mob go **to** the river.

Prepositions that show direction go with verbs of action and movement:

Flash **ran to** the water's edge

HMD **jumped up**.

Googal **walked along** the road.

How do I get to the Town Hall from here?
If I was going to the Town Hall, I wouldn't start from here.

Prepositions: Show location

4 All aboard

The Odd Mob decide to see if the raft will take them all.

The raft is moored **beside** the riverbank. The oil drums **under** the raft are keeping it afloat even though all the children are standing **on** it. Shagpile stays **in the middle** of the gang. She doesn't want another ducking!

Prepositions that tell you where something is, go with verbs describing how things are:

HMD **is on** the raft.
Googal saw a fish **in** the water.
The gang loves **being on** the river.

5 Let's play pirates

The Odd Mob are pretending to be pirates.

Prepositions: Show time

By the time the raft floats away from the riverbank, the Odd Mob has turned into a gang of pirates sailing on the *Spanish Main.*

They carry on with their swashbuckling **until** they see Mr Sumo watching them from a bridge. They have a funny feeling that it won't be long **before** they are in trouble.

Joke Break

Q: How do you recognise a stupid pirate?

A: He's got a patch over both eyes.

Mr Sumo has wanted to be a pirate ever **since** he was a child. **Before** the gang can stop him he leaps off the bridge.

After Mr Sumo boards the raft, the gang abandon ship. Poor old Mr Sumo is a nervous wreck **until** he finally finds the courage to wade ashore.

Prepositions of time show you when something happened:

at	**on**	**by**	**for**	**from**
since	**until**	**before**	**during**	**after**

6 The long arm of the law

The game's up for Mr Sumo.

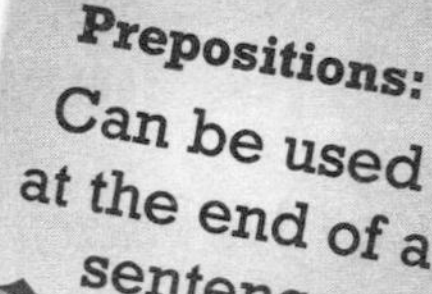

Prepositions:
Can be used at the end of a sentence

Mr Sumo's troubles aren't **over**. A police officer on patrol asks him what he thinks he's up **to**. The officer points at the river and makes Mr Sumo go back **in**. The would-be buccaneer has to struggle through the water and pull the sunken raft **out**.

Multiple Joyce

Which of these words is a preposition?

A Preposition
B Proposition
C Competition
D To

End a sentence with a preposition if it makes the sentence read more smoothly:

What are we waiting **for**?

For what are we waiting?

Is it any wonder the Odd Mob thinks Mr Sumo is a bit of a drip?

Conjunctions

The Museum Visit

Conjunctions: Connecting words

1 A rainy day

The Odd Mob are bored and want something to do.

Just our luck, it's Saturday **yet** it's raining.
And Ulf's broken the TV **so** I'm bored.
Well, we can sit here moaning **or** we can go to the museum.
I don't like the science stuff **but** I like the section on the Stone Age.
Yes, **but** you'll have to keep moving when we get there, Ulf, **or** people will think you're one of the exhibits!

The words **yet**, **or**, **but**, **for**, **and**, **nor**, **so** are called **co-ordinating conjunctions**. They link parts of sentences together.

Coordinating conjunctions link words and parts of sentences together:
Deej **and** Max were fed up.

Cheesy Chad says ...

Coordinating conjunctions don't add any extra information to a sentence.

② Food for thought

Correlative conjunctions:
Always work in pairs

The Odd Mob arrive at the museum. They're keen to go and see the exhibits but Mr Sumo has other things on his mind.

I **not only** want to see the dinosaur exhibits **but also** the section on Vikings.
I'll **either** see the Inca treasures **or** the knights in armour.
Neither of those interests me **nor** does stuff about the Victorians. I want to see the Egyptian mummies.
I don't know **whether** to have a cream cake **or** a fruit cake. I know! I'll have **both** of them **and** a chocolate éclair.
Exhibits
Tearoom

Joke Break

Q: When can a pair of big dinosaurs get under one umbrella and not get wet?

A: When it's not raining.

The most common correlative conjunctions are '**both** ... **and**', '**either** ... **or**', '**neither** ... **nor**', '**not only** ... **but also**', '**so** ... **as**' and '**whether** ... **or**'.

Correlative conjunctions work as a team to join similar ideas together:

Either Mr Sumo should go on a diet **or** he should get more exercise.

3 Does your mummy know you're here?

Subordinating conjunctions: Show less important ideas

HMD and Wozza have found their way into the mummy gallery.

Hey, Wozza, that mummy can't leave his case **because** he's all wrapped up.

Right! You should never cross an Egyptian mummy with a car mechanic **because** you'll get a toot and car man.

Hmm...it's lucky for HMD and Wozza that the mummy can't hear what they're saying or it might **cause** him to put a curse on them!

Subordinating conjunctions help the **less important idea** in a sentence to make sense:

The museum was spooky **because** the lights were dim.

4 A difference of opinion

Max and Deej have a falling out.

Opposing Conjunctions: Help make a discussion

These old suits of armour are cool **but** I thought the Inca treasure was more exciting.

That's your opinion. **However**, I disagree.

Oh, Deej, you say that, **though** you know nothing about history. I bet you don't even know where Hadrian's Wall is.
While you may think that, **nonetheless** you're wrong. Hadrian's Wall is round Hadrian's garden.
Why were the early days of history called the Dark Ages?

Because there were so many knights.

Here are some opposing conjunctions:

nevertheless **yet** **still**
nonetheless **although** **however**
though **whereas**

Opposing conjunctions are useful words to use when you're having a discussion:

Deej: **Although** you think the Vikings would beat the Romans in a fight, I think they wouldn't.

HMD: The Romans were hard but, **nevertheless**, the Vikings would still win.

⑤ What you see is what you get

Conjunctions of time: Tell when something happens

Ulf and Googal are admiring the dinosaurs.

Were people around **before** or **after** the dinosaurs?

The dinosaurs lived in an **earlier** period of history. People didn't come along **until** much **later**.

That's weird **since** for a **while** now I've been seeing a dinosaur with purple spots.

Really? Have you seen an eye doctor?

No, just a dinosaur with purple spots.

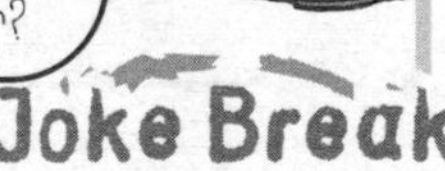

Q: What do you get when dinosaurs crash cars?

A: Tyrannosaurus Wrecks!

Here are some conjunctions of time:

before **after** **until** **as soon as**
till **while** **since** **when**

Conjuctions of time tell you when something has happened, is happening or will happen:

Ulf saw a dinosaur **earlier** today.

Now all is quiet.

But there'll be trouble **when** the dinosaur sees Ulf.

6 The ancient Greeks

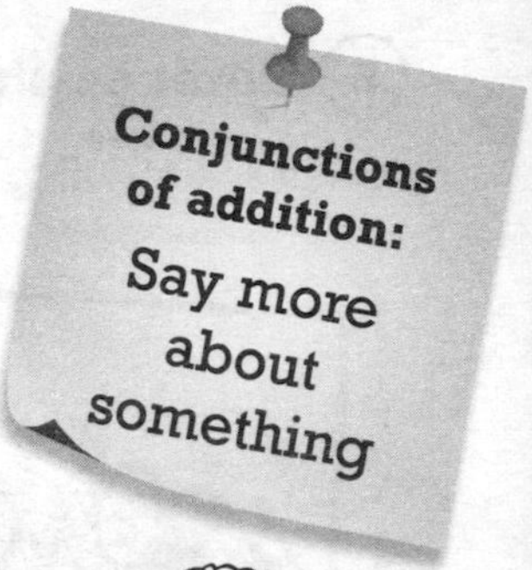

Flash and Shagpile find out about the first Olympic games.

Conjunctions of addition:
Say more about something

The ancient Greeks held the Olympic games at Mount Olympus. The athletes' aim was to honour the gods and **also** to win a laurel wreath. **Furthermore**, they wore no clothes when they ran.

Golly, that's too much information. How do you think the athletes must have felt after running a marathon stark naked, Shagpile?

Rrrrough!

Here are some conjunctions of addition:

furthermore **additionally** **also**

When you want to add information to what has been said or written, you can use **conjunctions of addition**:

Flash likes to run but she **also** likes to jump.

7 Back to the Stone Age

Oh dear, trust Ulf to do something silly.

The Odd Mob were enjoying the visit **until** Ulf joined the Stone Age people display.

The Odd Mob were enjoying the visit **because** Ulf joined the Stone Age people display.

The Odd Mob were enjoying the visit **so** Ulf joined the Stone Age people display.

The attendant didn't think Ulf's antics were funny **so** he told them to leave.

The attendant didn't think Ulf's antics were funny **until** he told them to leave.

It looks like museum visits are history for the gang from now on.

Multiple Joyce

Which of these words is a conjunction?

A so
B junction
C munchen
D function

Be careful when you use **conjunctions**. They can change what you mean to say:

Mr Sumo ate all the pies **until** he was overweight.
Mr Sumo ate all the pies **because** he was overweight.

Exclamations

The Vanishing Easter Egg Mystery

Exclamations: Express emotion

1 Emotions run high

I'm so **excited** about going egg rolling on Sunday!

Going egg rolling? You're weird and that **scares** me!

Don't be so **uptight**. I wouldn't egg-spect anything else of Wozza.

That's a dreadful pun and I absolutely **hate** bad puns!

I **love** a good row!

I get so **eggs-asperated** when the Odd Mob argue!

Emotions are starting to run high so Googal explains to the gang that egg rolling is an ancient custom where, to celebrate Easter Sunday, children roll painted eggs down a hillside. It's great fun! Try it – you'll **love** it!

An exclamation shows emotion:
Flash was really **delighted** with her Easter Egg!

2 The Odd Mob get over-egg-cited

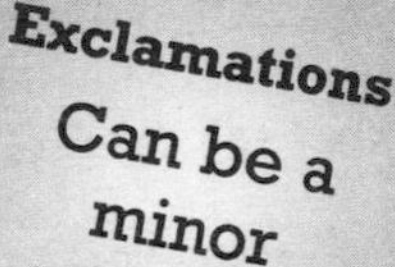

Googal has suggested that the Odd Mob enter the egg rolling competition.

The gang are so excited by Googal's suggestion that they've left out words from their sentences. For example, Deej thinks **it is** a great idea while HMD thinks **it is** far out. Max wants to do it **now**. Flash is in on this **idea** while Wozza **wants to take part** and Ulf thinks **this is the** way to go.

Joke Break

Q: What happens when you play table tennis with a bad egg?

A: First it goes ping – then it goes pong!

A **minor sentence** is one that has part of it left out to save repetition.

'What did you have for tea?'
'(I had) **An Easter egg.**'

Minor sentences can be used as exclamations:
Happy Easter! Good dog! Get lost! You're joking!

3 It's no eggs–aggeration!

The Odd Mob can't believe their eyes when they see the egg Ulf has brought along.

Exclamations:
Can be a single word

Wicked!

Egg-cellent!

Fantastic!

Brilliant!

Amazing!

Awesome!

Dinosaur!

I just hope the dinosaur who laid that egg doesn't come looking for it!

Humpty
Dumpty sat
on a wall
Humpty Dumpty
had a great fall
All the King's horses
and all the King's men
Had scrambled eggs for
breakfast again!

An **exclamation** is a word, phrase or sentence spoken with great feeling: '**What a whopper!**' yelled Deej.

(4) Egg roll!

The egg rolling competition begins …

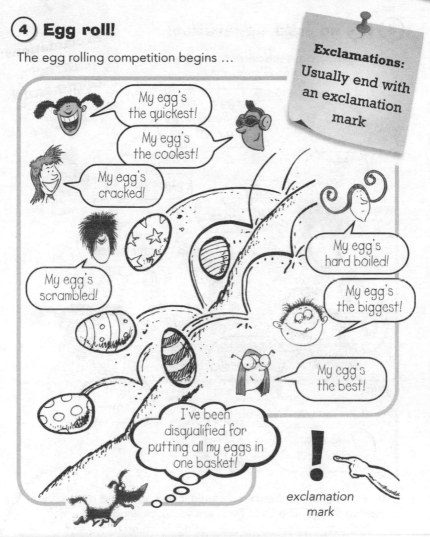

Exclamations:
Usually end with an exclamation mark

My egg's the quickest!

My egg's the coolest!

My egg's cracked!

My egg's scrambled!

My egg's hard boiled!

My egg's the biggest!

My egg's the best!

I've been disqualified for putting all my eggs in one basket!

!

exclamation mark

Some exclamations start with the words what or how:

What a beautiful day! How clever I am!

An **exclamation** usually has an **exclamation mark** at the end of it:

Goodness gracious me, that's eggs-traordinary!

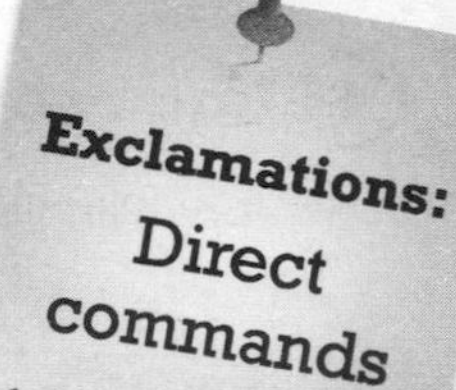

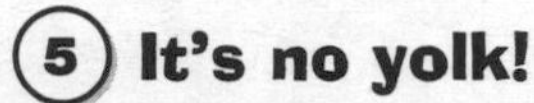

5 It's no yolk!

Ulf's dinosaur egg is missing!

My egg's gone missing. Somebody's stolen it!

Hunt them down!

Catch the crook!

Fetch the police!

Arrest someone!

Do it now!

Calm down, all of you!

Ulf's dinosaur egg has been stolen, but who would do such a terrible thing? The Odd Mob are so busy giving each other orders that they're not actually doing anything to track the thief down. They need to **wake up!**

An order or forceful command usually has an **exclamation mark** at the end of it:

Stop that thief!

⑥ You can't make an omelette

The egg thief is revealed!

Exclamations: Statements

These **exclamatory statements** all end with an **exclamation mark**. Unlike Mr Sumo, who's just come to a sticky end!

I'll teach you to eat my egg!

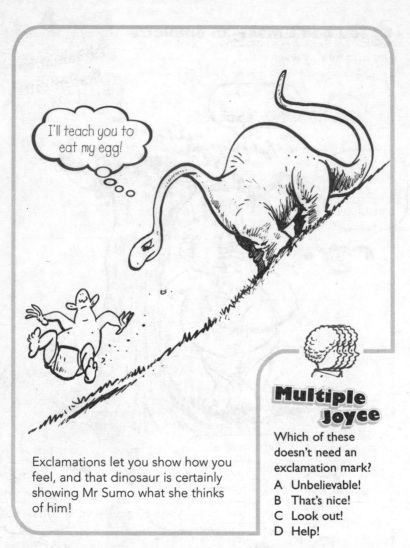

Exclamations let you show how you feel, and that dinosaur is certainly showing Mr Sumo what she thinks of him!

Multiple Joyce

Which of these doesn't need an exclamation mark?

A Unbelievable!
B That's nice!
C Look out!
D Help!

Some **exclamations** are like **statements**, but with an **exclamation mark** at the end instead of a full stop:

Mr Sumo is in big trouble!
Watch out, there's a dinosaur about!
I always knew Mr Sumo was a bad egg!

Sentences

The Haunted Cellar

Sentences:
Make sense on their own

1 A school for spooks

The Odd Mob's school is a bit creepy.

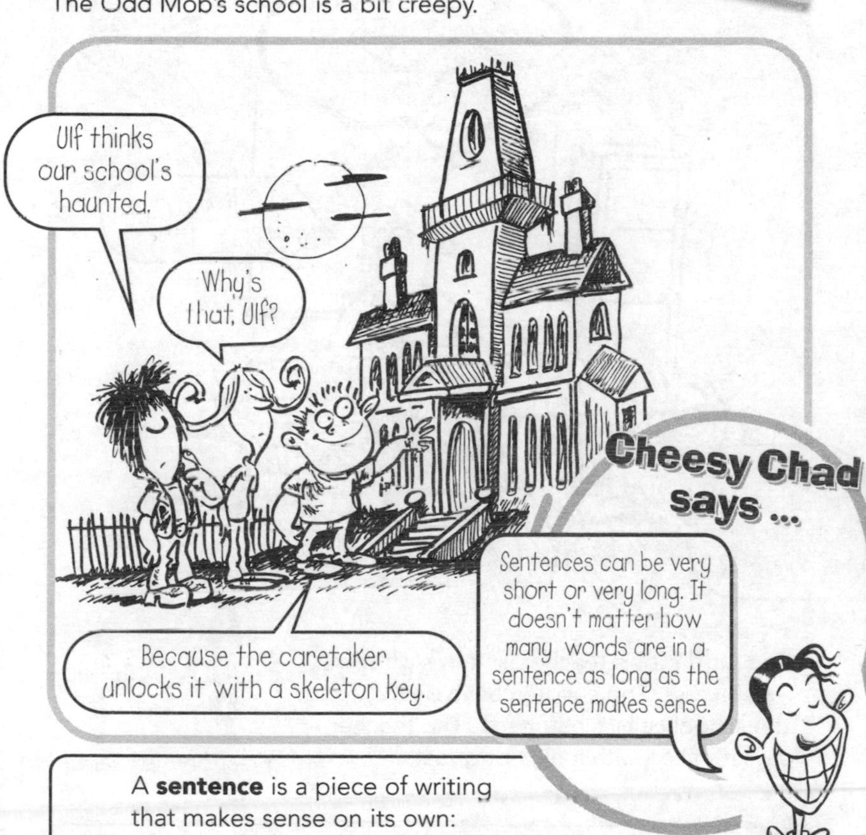

Ulf thinks our school's haunted.
Why's that, Ulf?
Because the caretaker unlocks it with a skeleton key.
Cheesy Chad says ...
Sentences can be very short or very long. It doesn't matter how many words are in a sentence as long as the sentence makes sense.

A **sentence** is a piece of writing that makes sense on its own:

The match was played in a good spirit. ✓
A sentence (makes sense)

Dog, laugh, butter next Thursday. ✗
Not a sentence (doesn't make sense)

2 Things that go bump in the night

There's a rumour going round that there's a ghost in the school cellar. The Odd Mob want to find out more about it so they ask their teacher.

Sentences:
Begin and end with the right punctuation

Is it true that the school cellar is haunted?

No, of course it isn't!

In my day, children weren't allowed to spook until they were spooken to.

The Odd Mob's teacher isn't in high spirits – he's cross**.** **T**he children have been saying the school cellar's haunted**!** **T**he teacher says it's filled with junk, not ghosts**.**

A *capital A*

. *full stop*

? *question mark*

! *exclamation mark*

A **sentence** begins with a **capital letter** and ends with a **full stop**, a **question mark** or an **exclamation mark**:

This is a skeleton joke**.**
Why didn't the skeleton go to the party**?**
It had no body to go with**!**

3 The school cellar

Sentences:
Have two parts: a subject and a predicate

The school cellar is a grim place.

The school cellar is huge and gloomy. **The Odd Mob** think it's haunted. **Their teacher** knows it isn't. It is filled with junk. Though, **that old bicycle** could do with some spooks in its wheels.

The **subject** is 'who' or 'what' the sentence is about. The **predicate** is all the rest of the sentence, e.g. The cellar (**the subject**) is filled with junk (the predicate).

A simple sentence is made up of a subject and a predicate:

Subject	**Predicate**
Wozza	asks a question
The teacher	is cross

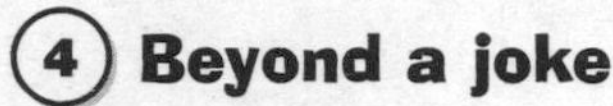

4 Beyond a joke

Deej and Wozza get the giggles.

Sentences: Must have a verb

What kind of ghost has the best hearing?

The eeriest.

Deej and Wozza **upset** the teacher by telling each other ghost jokes.

A **verb** is a 'doing' or 'being' word. For example, in the sentence 'Ulf **sees** a ghost and **hides** behind the sofa', '**sees**' and '**hides**' are verbs.

A **sentence** always has a **verb**:
The ghost **floated** in the air.
Ulf **screamed** loudly.
The ghost **flew** away.

(5) Laying down the law

Imperative Sentences: Are commands

The Odd Mob are convinced that there is something strange about the school cellar. They keep on about it until their teacher loses patience with them.

Stop asking daft questions about the school cellar! And **don't** try to sneak down into the cellar. I **forbid** it!
Don't shout so loud - you'll wake the dead!
Cheesy Chad says ...
There are four types of sentence: imperative, interrogative, exclamatory and declarative.

Imperative sentences tell you what to do or what not to do:

Listen to me.
Don't go down in the woods today.

6 A question of nerve

Out in the playground at break time the Odd Mob continue the discussion.

Interrogative sentences: Ask questions
Max, do you have the nerve to go in the haunted cellar?
No, do you?
What about if you took Shagpile with you?
Hmm ... am I a dog or a chicken?
Hey, who laid this egg?

The gang want to see if the cellar really is haunted, but are any of them brave enough to risk going down into it?

Joke Break

Q: What do you call a dating agency for ghosts?

A: Love at first fright!

Interrogative sentences often begin with a **question** word such as **what**, **who**, **how**, **why** or **when**.

Interrogative sentences ask for information and end with a **question mark**:

Why do you think the cellar's haunted?

7 Curiosity killed the cat

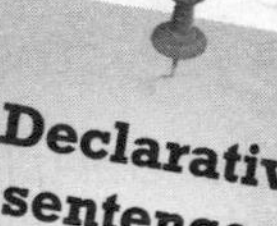

Declarative sentences:
Make statements

Flash and Ulf decide that they have to find out what is inside the cellar.

I'll go down into the cellar.

Me too.

You're so brave.

You're so daft.

You're so cool.

You're soooo in trouble.

Joke Break

Q: Why doesn't Dracula have any friends?

A: Because he's a pain in the neck!

A **declarative** sentence simply states a fact or an argument:
The cellar is dark.

8 To boldly go

Flash and Ulf have sneaked down into the school cellar.

Exclamatory sentences:
Express strong feelings
It's totally scary down here!
I really wish I'd brought a torch!
These kids must be bats!
I can see a bat.
Leave it. I don't like cricket!

Golly, the cellar is dark and creepy!
It's no wonder Flash and Ulf are jumpy!

Exclamatory sentences always end with **exclamation marks**. So don't forget that!

An **exclamatory** sentence is a more powerful type of declarative sentence:
Ulf and Flash were terrified of the skeleton!

9 It's a nightmare!

Compound sentences: Two or more simple sentences joined together

Ulf and Flash race back to tell their teacher what's happened.

You said the cellar wasn't haunted but that isn't true.

We saw a ghost but I jumped on it and I smashed it.

You've both been dreaming or you're making this up!

Actually, I was going to haunt the cellar but it's too scary down there for me.

And, **but**, **or** are the conjunctions that join simple sentences together and turn them into **compound** sentences.

A **compound** sentence is made by joining two simple sentences together with a **conjunction** (joining word):

Ulf opened the door **and** Flash shone her torch into the room.

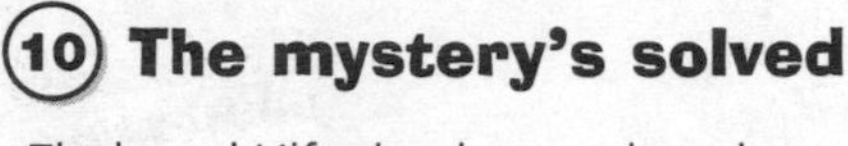

(10) The mystery's solved

Complex Sentences:
Have a subordinate clause

Flash and Ulf take the teacher down to the cellar to show him the skeleton.

We didn't believe in ghosts **until we were attacked by that.**

You're both in trouble now **because that's not a ghost!**

Yes it is, **unless** you know better?

Since **you ask**, it's a plastic skeleton I use for teaching biology lessons!

Doh!

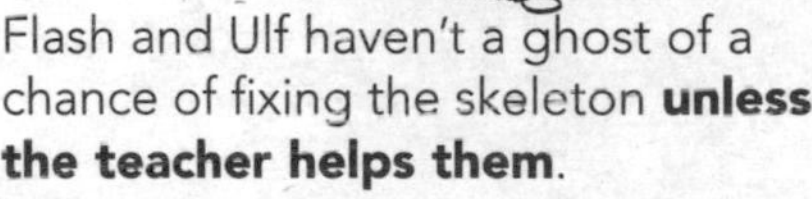

Flash and Ulf haven't a ghost of a chance of fixing the skeleton **unless the teacher helps them**.

Multiple Joyce

Which of these is a sentence?

A I saw a ghost.
B Eating toast.
C Halfway up a lamp post.
D Whoo!

A **subordinate clause** starts with a conjunction and needs a main clause to go with it:

Although it was only made of plastic, the skeleton was scary.

A subordinate clause doesn't make sense on its own:

Ulf and Flash were brave **until they saw the skeleton**.
The cellar isn't haunted **although the children thought it was**.

Phrases

Football Crazy

Phrases:
A group of words

1 Team talk

The Odd Mob are challenged to a game of footy by a rival gang, Rudy's Rabble. They have a meeting to discuss tactics.

'**For a change**' does not make sense on its own. It is a **phrase**.

Each set of words in bold is a phrase.

A phrase is a group of words which does not make sense on its own:

with a friend **middle chair** **just like two old men**

Phrases:
Not sentences

2 Sails pitch

It's the afternoon of the big footy match. The gang are having a bit of trouble finding the pitch.

I thought the pitch was **down there**.

It's **across this road**, isn't it?

No, we need to look **behind those tall trees**.

Someone told me it was **near this muddy lake**.

It is **this muddy lake**!

Oh, hello, Rudy ...

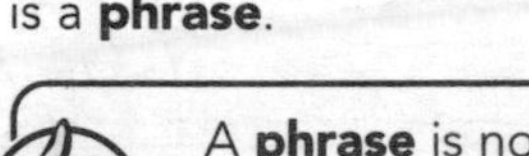

Whoops! Each set of words in bold is a **phrase**.

Smith was a dangerous player ...

A **phrase** is not a sentence because it doesn't make sense on its own:

across this road **dangerous player** **with a smile**

Phrases:
Do not contain a verb

3 You mark the big lad

The two teams line up for the big match: The Odd Mob v Rudy's Rabble.

They're all **ten feet tall**!

Rudy's whole team are monsters!

We're going to get mashed **to a pulp**!

Cheesy Chad says ...

Sometimes people use the word 'phrase' to mean an expression such as 'get real'.

Things don't look good. Deej, HMD and Max have each used a **phrase** to describe something.

A phrase does not contain a verb (action):

in the lake **a great big player** **all over**

4 Goal fest

The big match is finally underway. But it's not going well for the Odd Mob ...

Phrases: Some phrases are overused

Easy as pie: that's 10-0!

My brain aches.

That was a rocket shot!

We need a goalie as big as a giant.

Joke Break

Mick: Why is the footy pitch at Wembley a triangle?

Rick: Someone took a corner.

It's football but the Odd Mob are facing a cricket score.

And some of their phrases are ones which are **overused** – they are **clichés**.

Some well-known football expressions are called clichés because they're used too often:

a game of two halves **sick as a parrot**
I'm over the moon

Phrases: Add interest to sentences

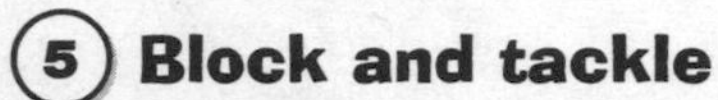

5 Block and tackle

It looks like the gang have solved their goalkeeping crisis with a late team change ...

It's the first time in **living memory** that Mr Sumo's ever been helpful!
And it's good that Flash scored those 11 goals too - **a real stroke of luck.**
What a game...

Rudy's phrase sums up that match! Googal's and Deej's phrases add **extra interest** to what they say.

Which of these is not a phrase?

A A change of luck
B A change of underpants
C Change your goalie.
D Strange, your goalie

Phrases can make dull sentences more interesting:

The game, **a battle of giants**, was won 11-10 by the Odd Mob.

Clauses

No sanity clause

Clauses: are the building blocks of sentences

1 Christmas is coming

The Odd Mob have got the wrong idea about clauses.

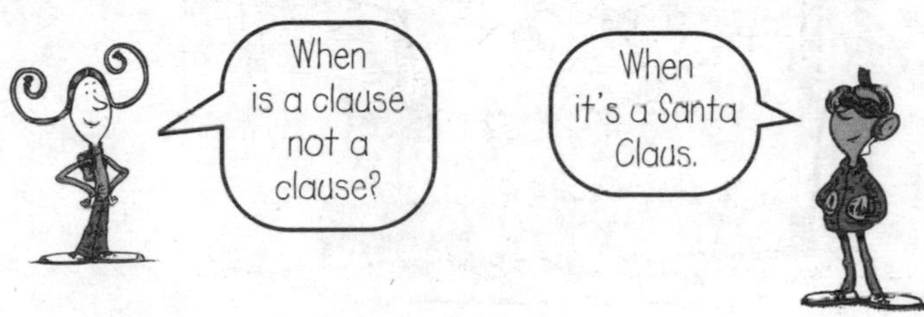

When is a clause not a clause?
When it's a Santa Claus.

The Odd Mob are studying **clauses** for English homework. They're getting things all muddled up. They think **clauses** wear red coats, have big white beards and say, 'Ho! Ho! Ho!' Googal soon puts them right. She tells them that Santa Claus is another name for Father Christmas, while a **clause** is a distinct part of a sentence.

There are two types of clauses: main clauses and dependent clauses.

A clause isn't a jolly fat man - it's part of a sentence.

Every sentence is made up of one or more clauses:

Deej is a good boy, but not always.

(main clause) (dependent clause)

Clauses:
Main clauses make sense on their own

2 Ulf is confused

Ulf needs more clues about clauses.

What do you call people who are afraid of Santa Claus?

Claustrophobic!

I don't get this stuff about Santa clauses.

A main clause is the key part of a sentence. It makes sense on its own. For example:

Despite what Googal said about clauses, **Ulf is still confused**. Mind you, it doesn't help when **HMD and Deej keep making corny jokes about Father Christmas**. **Ulf walks away** because he has an idea of how he can find out about clauses for himself.

Joke Break

Q: What do you call a cat on a beach at Christmas time?

A: Sandy claws

A main clause makes sense by itself:

A vampire snowman gives you a frost bite when you meet it.

(Main clause)

③ Poles apart

Ulf is off on a quest to find Santa Claus.

Clauses:
Dependent clauses don't make sense by themselves

Ulf has set off for the North Pole **because that's where he thinks Father Christmas lives**. **Ulf reckons that with a name like Claus**, Santa knows all about clauses. **Before he has gone very far**, Ulf spots a banner hanging across a big store window. Ulf's really surprised **when he sees this**. **Until he saw the sign**, Ulf had no idea the North Pole was in a shop in his home town.

Joke Break

Q: Where do you find reindeer?

A: I dunno – it depends where you left them.

A **dependent clause** only makes sense when linked with the main clause:

Ulf went to see Father Christmas **when he had some free time**.

(Dependent clause)

4 The grotty grotto

Clauses:
A dependent clause gives more information

Ulf goes into Santa's grotto.

Before he can go in to see Santa, Ulf has to stand in a long queue. **Because he wants to be the first to see Santa**, Ulf decides to sneak into the grotto. **Although he is being naughty**, Ulf is sure no one will see him.

A **dependent clause** tells you more about the main clause:

If he sees Santa, Ulf knows he will be given a present.

5 He's going to find out who's naughty ...

Ulf meets Santa Claus.

Clauses:
Clauses can be linked together by conjunctions

Ulf tells Santa that he's been good all year, though he hasn't really. Santa says he'll give Ulf a present **because** Ulf has been a good boy.

Hmm ... it doesn't seem right that Ulf is tricking Santa Claus, **although** there is something suspiciously familiar about this Father Christmas.

Joke Break

Q: What's the best Christmas present in the world?

A: A broken drum – you just can't beat it!

A **conjunction** can be used to join **clauses** together:
Ulf was feeling guilty **because** he told Santa Claus a fib.

⑥ Scrooge not Santa Claus

Clauses:
How to spot a clause (and a dodgy Santa)

Ulf saves Santa.

Ulf **falls** off Santa's knee and **grabs** at Santa's beard. *It* **peels** off and *Ulf* **discovers** Santa is actually *Mr Sumo* in disguise! Mr Sumo **has tied** up the real Santa and **hidden** him behind Santa's throne. Mr Sumo was going to steal all the children's presents. Luckily *Ulf* **has foiled** his wicked plan.

Multiple Joyce

Which of these is a clause?

A Santa Claus
B Claustrophobia
C Claws
D It's a get-out clause.

All clauses have a *subject* and a **verb**:

Mr Sumo **ran** away. ✓ This is a clause because it has a subject (Mr Sumo) and a verb (ran).

Leaving behind the presents. ✗
This is not a clause. It has a verb (leaving) but no subject.

Ho, ho, ho! ✗ This is not a clause because it doesn't have a subject or a verb.

Paragraphs

Dangerous Sports Special!

Paragraphs: Groups of sentences

1 Hang-gliding hiccup

Deej has to write about sports for his homework. He's chosen five dangerous sports and goes to watch them with Googal.

First they watch Ulf and Max go hang gliding.

What is hang gliding?

You basically jump off a hill or mountain and glide down.

Ulf! I think you've forgotten something.

Wheee!

Deej has to organise his writing into paragraphs.

Paragraph

Dangerous Sports

Hang gliding is a sport. You basically jump off a hill or a mountain and glide down. It's quite dangerous.

A **paragraph** is a group of sentences about one **subject** or **idea**.

② Stark raving mud

Paragraphs: Help organise writing

Next, Deej and Googal go to watch Wozza try dirt-bike racing to help with Deej's homework.

Why does my work need to be in paragraphs?

It helps to make your writing clear to the reader. Writing is easier to follow when it's organised into sections. But where's Wozza?

That was fun.

Afterwards, Deej's writing looked like this – it had two paragraphs.

Dangerous Sports

Hang gliding is a sport. You basically jump off a hill or a mountain and glide down. It's quite dangerous. — About hang gliding

Dirt-bike racing is another dangerous sport. You ride a motorbike through lots of mud and dirt. — About dirt bikes

A **paragraph** can be **short** or **long**.

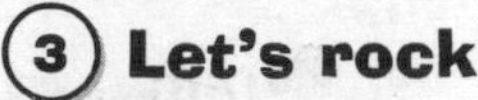

3 Let's rock

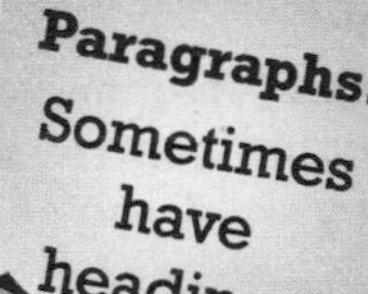

Deej is still struggling to write about dangerous sports. He goes with Googal to see Flash try rock climbing for some ideas.

Won't all these ropes get in the way when I run up?

Here is Deej's paragraph about rock climbing. It has a heading.

Rock climbing

Rock climbing is one of the most dangerous sports in the world. A lot of equipment is needed, such as helmets, ropes and harnesses. Rock climbers also wear special shoes to give them a good grip.

In non-fiction or informational writing, **paragraphs** sometimes have **headings**.

④ One two free fall

Paragraphs: Used for breaks and dialogue

Deej's homework on dangerous sports is going well. He and Googal go to watch HMD try sky-diving next.

Hey, that's given me an idea for a story!

Well, if you write fiction, you need a new paragraph each time there's a new speaker. You also start a new paragraph where there's a change of time or place.

Cheesy Chad says ...

You need a new paragraph to introduce a new person too.

In **fiction** a new **paragraph** is used:

- where there is a **natural break** in the story
- where there is **dialogue** (speech)

5 Bully for you

Deej and Googal look at one last dangerous sport: they go to see Mr Sumo try bull riding.

Paragraphs:
Indent the first word

I didn't realise it was dangerous for the bull!

Don't forget to write a paragraph on this – and get a picture!

Dangerous Sports

Indent

Bull riding is another dangerous sport. Unlucky bulls get dangerously heavy riders like Mr Sumo. It's hard to breathe with an elephant on your back.

What is an indent?

A The opposite of an outdent
B A gap
C A small tooth
D I've no idea

The first word of a **paragraph** is normally **indented**.

Word Order

Watch the birdie!

Word order: Be careful placing adverbs

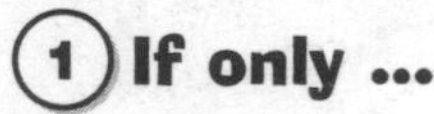

If only ...

The gang decide to go bird watching at the local pond.

Only HMD went bird watching with a guitar.

Hang on a minute. Does it matter where we put the adverb 'only' in the sentence above?

Yes! Compare these:

1 HMD **only** went bird watching with a guitar.
2 HMD went bird watching with a guitar **only**.
3 **Only** HMD went bird watching with a guitar.
4 HMD went **only** bird watching with a guitar.

They're quite different, eh?

The position of an adverb in a sentence is important:
Just Ulf went out. Ulf **just** went out.

There were lots [folded] ...ting birds to see at the pond.

Max saw a heron looking through binoculars.

Hey! That's not right! You mean
Looking through a pair of binoculars, Max saw a heron.

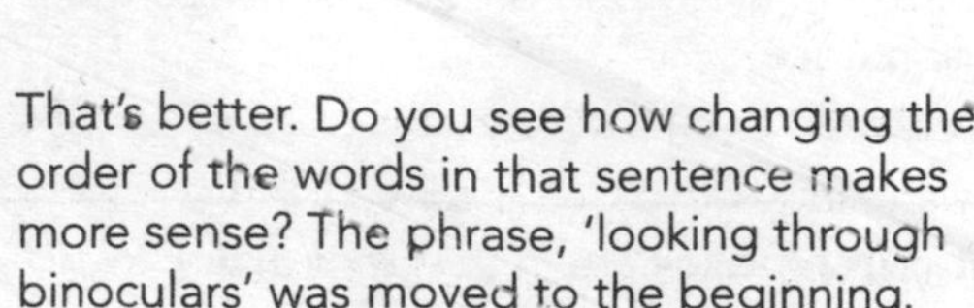

That's better. Do you see how changing the order of the words in that sentence makes more sense? The phrase, 'looking through binoculars' was moved to the beginning.

Bullfinch

Phrases in the wrong place can make a sentence very odd:

Max saw a man fishing with an umbrella.
Max saw a man with an umbrella fishing.

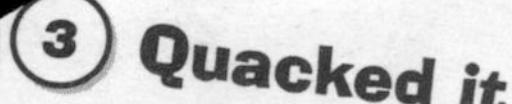

3 Quacked it

Word order: Moving phrases changes meaning

Deej wants to feed the ducks at the

Deej has some bread for th
ducks in his pocket.

I thi
something's
wrong here.
It should be 'Deej has some bread in his pocket for the ducks.'

Putting words or a phrase in the wrong order can change the whole meaning of a sentence.

Make sure that your **phrases** are in the right **order** to avoid confusion:

Flash kept some bugs she found in a box.

Did she find the bugs in the box?

Did she find them somewhere else and then put them in the box?

Who knows!

4 Beware: low-flying trees

The Odd Mob have a great time spotting birds and, er, other things by the pond.

YOU CAN DO IT!

Wat... order o... clauses

I heard that Ulf saw two swans near the trees that were flying.

What! The trees were flying?

Er, I think he meant that he saw two swans that were flying by the trees.

Mmm ... he separated the **clause** 'that were flying' from the **subject**, the swans.

Cheesy Chad says ...

Read your sentences aloud if you're not sure about the word order.

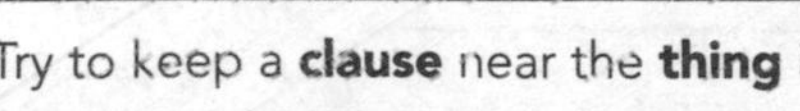

Try to keep a **clause** near the **thing** it describes:

Deej gave some **bread** to a duck **that was well buttered**. ✗

Deej gave some **bread that was well buttered** to a duck. ✓

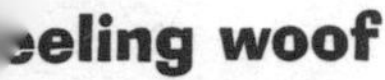

…eeling woof

… long walk home from the pond for … gang.

Word order:
Make yourself clear

Did you see that? Shagpile was chasing a kid on a skateboard!

But who was on the skateboard, the kid or Shagpile?

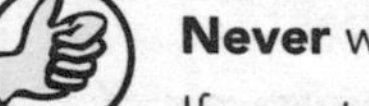

Never write:

If your trousers are dirty, you can drop them at the dry cleaners.

Multiple Joyce

Which of these bits of Shakespeare are in the right order?

A To be or not to be.
B Not be to or be to
C 2B not to be.
D Do be do be do.

Words Often Confused

Time-travel trauma

Mix-up alert:
of
off

1 Heading for Henry

Deej and Max have built a cunning time machine (as you do). They hope to explore the future …

You've pressed one **of** the wrong switches!

I can't turn it **off**!

… but they ended up in 1542!

Off with their heads!

Let's get out **of** here, pronto!

Of sounds like 'ov'. **Off** is the opposite of 'on'.

2 A pair of losers

Max and Deej are back in their time machine.

Mix-up alert:
lose
loose

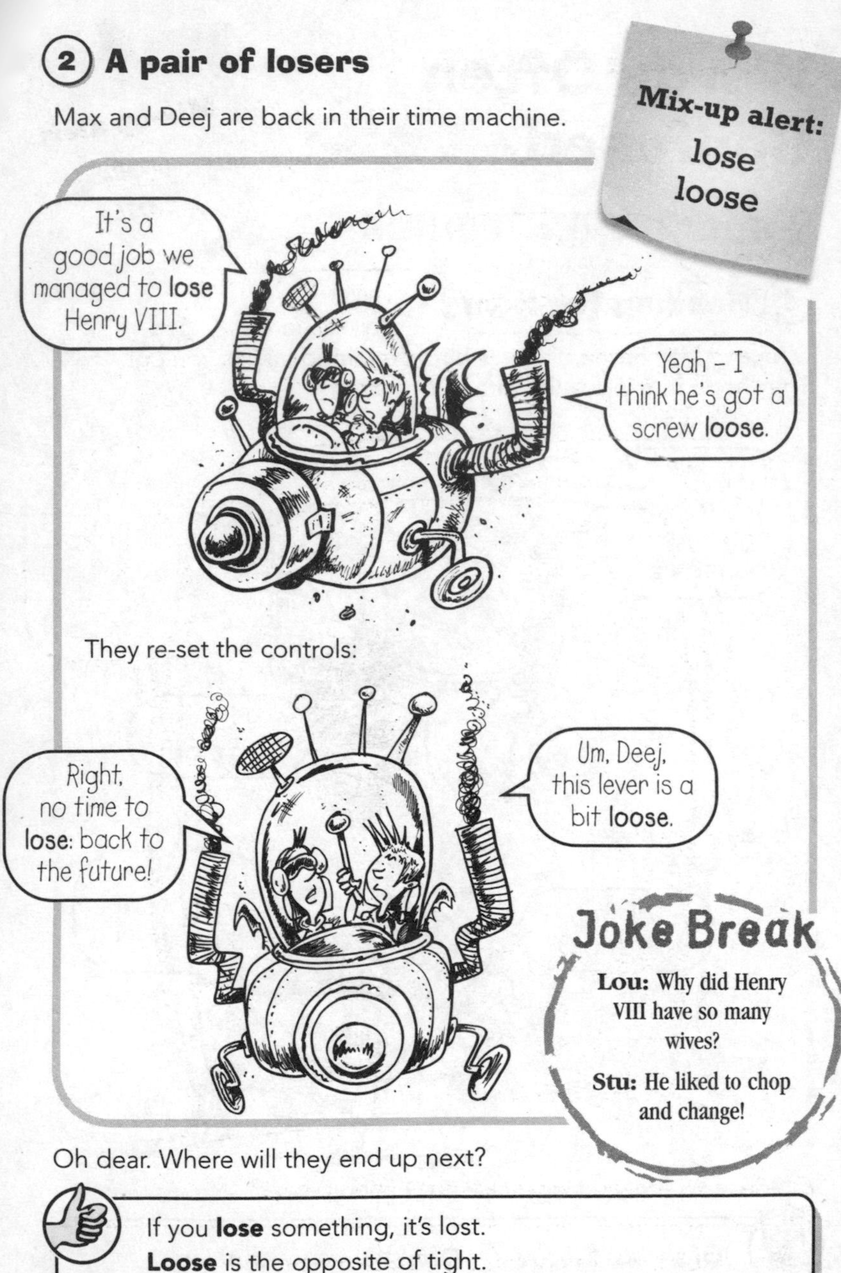

It's a good job we managed to **lose** Henry VIII.
Yeah – I think he's got a screw **loose**.
Right, no time to **lose**: back to the future!
Um, Deej, this lever is a bit **loose**.

They re-set the controls:

Joke Break

Lou: Why did Henry VIII have so many wives?

Stu: He liked to chop and change!

Oh dear. Where will they end up next?

If you **lose** something, it's lost.
Loose is the opposite of tight.

3 It's like a cave, man

The time machine made by Max and Deej has landed somewhere … but where? And when?

Mix-up alert:
quite
quiet

It's very **quiet** here, Max – no people about.
These trees are **quite** unusual too.
Ulf's here! You're being **quiet** today, Ulf.
You don't **quite** understand, Deej, this is NOT the future!

Oh dear. Where (and when) will they end up next?

Quiet means not loud. **Quite** rhymes with bite.

4 Roman round

Max and Deej are still busy time travelling …

Mix-up alert:
your
you're
You're a rubbish driver, Deej – this isn't the year 3000.
Never mind – this might help with **your** history homework.
Friends, Romans, countrymen, lend me **your** ears.
You're not having my ears, but you can borrow these headphones if you want.

A pair of Caesars

They have to leave, very quickly, again …

Your things belong to you. **You're** is short for 'you are'.

5 Meet some old timers

Mix-up alert:
are
our

At last, time travellers Deej and Max make it into the future.

Too freaky! It's back to the time machine, rapido!

Our things belong to us.

Are and **our** are totally different!

6 Time to go home

After that fright, Max and Deej just want to go home. But things don't go well …

First of all, the time machine's **brake** started to **break**, so they couldn't slow down.

'We're going faster than the machine's **allowed!**' Max screamed **aloud**.

Just when it was time to eat **dessert**, they crashed in a **desert!**

Cheesy Chad says …

Learn the difference. And never try to cross a dessert on a camel …

brake – to stop

break – something gets broken

aloud – with noise

allowed – if someone allows you

dessert – pud

desert – a hot and dry place

7 Everyone likes a present

Deej and Max are finally home ...

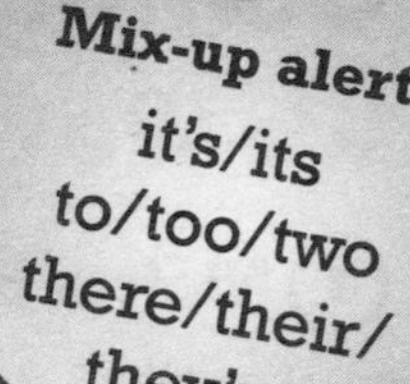

There are times when **they're** glad to be back in **their** home, in the present day.

It's the end of their adventures because the time machine broke when **its** engine fell out.

Anyway, these **two** kids are far **too** tired **to** go time travelling again.

Multiple Joyce

Which of these is correct?

A To blind mice
B Too blind mice
C Two blind mice
D Five deaf hamsters

'Its' is used when something **belongs** to something else.

Their also shows that something **belongs** to some people or some things.

it's – it is **they're** – they are **two** – 2

Common Mistakes

We Woz Robbed!

Common mistake: them/those

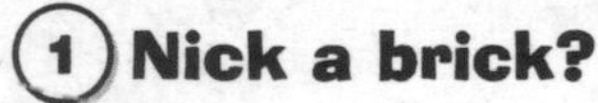

1 Nick a brick?

Deej and Googal are walking home one night when ...

Right, kiddies – give us all your money. We're going clubbing!

But we've only got 1p.

Well, give us **them** headphones, then.

You mean, 'Give us **those** headphones.'

Yer what?

Those headphones is correct English, not **them** headphones.

Dunno what you're on about. What's in **them** two bags?

There's nothing much in **those** bags except my mobile – but it's quite old.

A mobile? Give it here.

Well, OK.

Don't get mixed up with the words **them** and **those**:

Deej likes **them** big old mobiles. ✗

Deej likes **those** big old mobiles. ✓

2 A spot of bother

The muggers got away with Deej's headphones!

Common mistake: of/have

Yeah, my headphones are gone. It could **of** been worse – they might **of** hurt us. Maybe we should **of** run away. Anyway, the police might catch them – they won't **of** got far.

DEEJ! That's such bad grammar!

- It could **have** been worse.
- They might **have** hurt us.
- We should **have** run away.
- They won't **have** got far.

Robber gloves

Watch out! Many people use **of** when they mean **have**:

The robbery could **of** been nasty. ✗

The robbery could **have** been nasty. ✓

3 Write or wrong?

Googal and Deej have to make a statement at the police station.

Common mistake:
stood/standing
sat/sitting

Deej and Googal write down what happened:

Name: *Deej* Date: *28.1.11*

*We were **stood** on the street when two massive big lads came and nicked my headphones. Luckily I have another 28 pairs at home.*
*After that we told the police and we've been **sat** here for hours.*

Joke Break

Mo: Why did the crab blush?

Flo: Because the sea weed.

Just holding up the traffic, sarge

Name: *Googal* Date: *28.1.11*

We were **standing** on the pavement when a pair of remarkably hefty male individuals came and pilfered Deej's Sony HB9117 headphones. Fortunately, he possesses many others. Following the situation we informed the police and have been **sitting** here for a lengthy period.

Cheesy Chad says ...

Notice any differences there? Well, there are a few, yes.

But which is right:

'We were **stood**' or
'We were **standing**'?

The second one!
At least Deej got the date right ...

It's OK to say or write, 'I stood in the street', or 'I sat on a pie'. Just don't use 'was' in there!

Try not to use **stood** or **sat** wrongly:

They were **sat** in the police station. ✗

They were **sitting** in the police station. ✓

They **sat** in the police station. ✓

4 Repetition mission

Common mistake: Repeating yourself

HMD heard about the robbery and told the rest of the gang.

I think he may have got one or two facts wrong …

These five robbers with axes and flamethrowers chased Deej and Goog for miles. Then they cornered them in a dark alley. Then the men took everything off them: bags, watches, phones, clothes – the lot. Then Goog and Deej ran away in the nuddy. Then the police came then a SWAT team arrived then the Army then the gang were caught with giant nets.

The gang agreed on two things:

1. HMD's story was rubbish.
2. He kept repeating himself. He used the word **then** seven times! That is sooooo boring.

When speaking or writing, try not to **repeat** words several times:

then … then … then   and … and … and
said … said … said

5 You're nicked!

Common mistake: Using double negatives

A few days later, down at the police station …

We didn't rob nobody!
I'm not saying nothing.

Oh dear, not only are these two a pair of rotten criminals but their English is pants!

The first one said, 'We **didn't** rob **nobody!**' but he doesn't mean that. He's using a **double negative**. What he means is:

'We didn't rob anybody.' **or** 'We robbed nobody.'

The second one is using a double negative too. He said, 'I'm not saying nothing.' What he really means is:

'I'm not saying anything.' **or** 'I'm saying nothing.'

Anyway, they're both lying!

When speaking or writing, try not to use double negatives:

You don't know nothing. ✗ You don't know anything. ✓

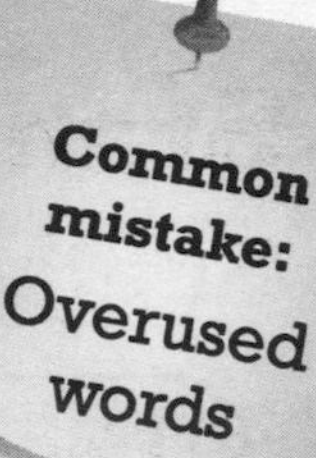
Common mistake: Overused words

⑥ Who get got?

A week after the robbery, Max is reading the local newspaper.

Here's the report.

Robbers get got

Two **bad** robbers were put in jail today after stealing some **cool** headphones from **good** gang members Deej and Googal. This is **absolutely great** news for these **nice** kids. The robbers were caught after **brilliant** work by the police.

Max was shocked:

Look at all of the overused words they wrote! I've highlighted them.

Ugh! Even I could do better than that.

Hang on – it wasn't that bad ...

Multiple Joyce

Which of these words is overused?

A got
B dimple
C overused
D perspicacity

Try not to use these words when you write. They're used too much:

get good cool nice great got

Standard English

Get the Message!

Standard English: Sometimes called formal English

1 Piece of pie

Wozza has won a competition in the local newspaper. Her prize is to write a report about her hobby, collecting pies. That night, she goes on Messenga instant messaging to ask the gang for help.

Fill me with pies

Come on you reds

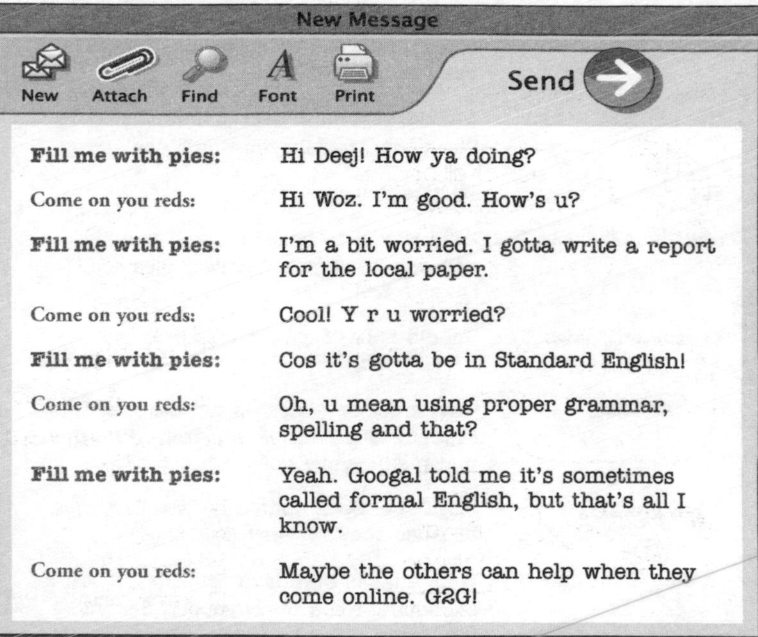

Fill me with pies:	Hi Deej! How ya doing?
Come on you reds:	Hi Woz. I'm good. How's u?
Fill me with pies:	I'm a bit worried. I gotta write a report for the local paper.
Come on you reds:	Cool! Y r u worried?
Fill me with pies:	Cos it's gotta be in Standard English!
Come on you reds:	Oh, u mean using proper grammar, spelling and that?
Fill me with pies:	Yeah. Googal told me it's sometimes called formal English, but that's all I know.
Come on you reds:	Maybe the others can help when they come online. G2G!

Standard English is formal **written** and **spoken** English. It is the English taught in **schools**.

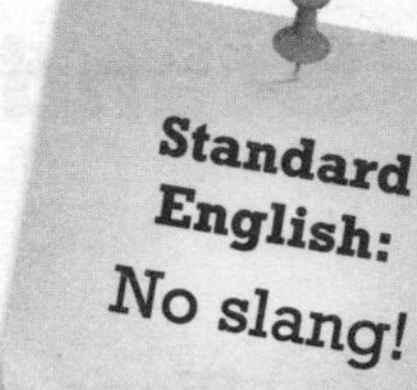

2 Nil bril

Max is the next one to sign into Messenga – can she help Wozza to understand what Standard English is?

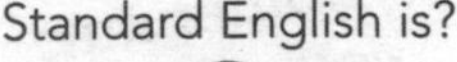

Fill me with pies

Live life to the max

New Message

New | Attach | Find | Font | Print | Send

Live life to the max:	Hi Woz. I got a text from Deej. He says you're a reporter now!
Fill me with pies:	Hi Max! Yeah, I have to write a news report on pies using Standard English but I'm a bit stuck.
Live life to the max:	I asked my mum and she says that in Standard English you don't use slang.
Fill me with pies:	What d'you mean?
Live life to the max:	Well, if you're writing about pies you shouldn't put 'I collect pies cos they're bril.'
Fill me with pies:	Should it be 'I collect pies because they're bril.'?
Live life to the max:	That's better – 'cos' is not Standard English, but neither is using 'bril' when you mean 'very good'.
Fill me with pies:	Oh, I see. So it should be 'I collect pies because they're very good.'
Live life to the max:	Well, that is Standard English but it's a bit boring for a news report! See ya – GTG xxx.

Standard English does not contain **slang**.

3 Accents will happen

A few minutes later, HMD signs in on Messenga

Fill me with pies

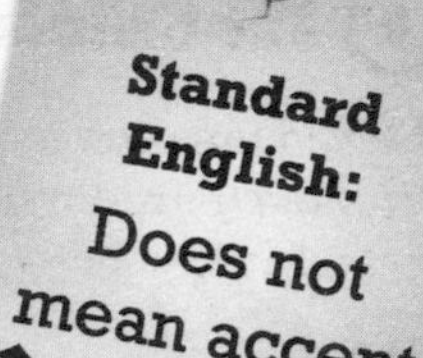

The Hairy Axeman

Standard English: Does not mean accent

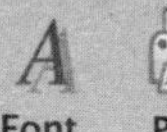

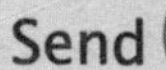

Fill me with pies:	Hi HMD. Wassup?
The Hairy Axeman:	Yo Wozza! I hear you need help with Standard English.
Fill me with pies:	Yeah – I gotta write a newspaper report for a competition.
The Hairy Axeman:	Right, I see. Well I know that Standard English is nothing to do with accents.
Fill me with pies:	You mean how people pronounce words?
The Hairy Axeman:	Yeah. People from all over the country and the world speak and write Standard English. It's more to do with choosing words which are widely thought of as correct.
Fill me with pies:	You mean posh?
The Hairy Axeman:	No, it's not posh. It's just supposed to be clear, so that everyone can understand it.
Fill me with pies:	Thanks HMD – I'm beginning to see now.
The Hairy Axeman:	No worries, dude. (That's not Standard English!) Bye.

Standard English is nothing to do with **accent**.
It doesn't mean **posh!**

4 That's news to me

Standard English:
For important communications

Next, Flash comes online, and chats to Wozza by instant messaging.

Fill me with pies

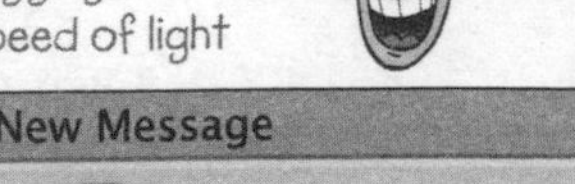

Jogging at the speed of light

New Message

New Attach Find Font Print Send

Fill me with pies:	Hi Flash! Have you heard about my news article too?
Jogging at the speed of light:	Hiya! Sure have – I just saw Max. She said you have to write about pies.
Fill me with pies:	True, but it's all gotta be in Standard English.
Jogging at the speed of light:	Right – can't use 'gotta' then, for a start ... my dad's a newsreader for local radio – he uses Standard English all the time.
Fill me with pies:	Why?
Jogging at the speed of light:	It's used for anything important, like news or traffic announcements.
Fill me with pies:	I see – but when is it used in writing?
Jogging at the speed of light:	You would use it for important writing such as business letters, job applications, essays or health warnings.
Fill me with pies:	Right – and newspaper reports too ...
Jogging at the speed of light:	That's it. You'll do fine, Woz! G2G.

Standard English is used for important written or spoken communications:

essays news reports job letters official notices

5 Pie panic!

Now Googal and Ulf sign into Messenga.

Standard English: Follows accepted rules

Fill me with pies

Know it, don't blow it

Urrgghhug!

New Message

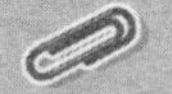

Send 

Know it, don't blow it:	Hi Wozza. Hi Ulf.
Fill me with pies:	Hi.
Urrgghhug!:	What's this about pies?
Fill me with pies:	I have to write about pies using Standard English.
Know it, don't blow it:	Oh, that's easy. Standard English just uses all the accepted rules of grammar, spelling and vocabulary.
Urrgghhug!:	Eh?
Fill me with pies:	I know – everyone's been helping me.
Know it, don't blow it:	Excellent! Just use good, clear formal English with no slang or 'street-speak'.
Fill me with pies:	Great – I can do that. G2G and write this report now – bye!
Urrgghhug!:	Hey! BUT WHAT ABOUT THE PIES?

Multiple Joyce

Which of these phrases is Standard English?

A I'm gutted.
B It's a disappointment.
C Drat!
D Un, deux, trois.

Standard English uses widely accepted rules of grammar, spelling and vocabulary, as explained in this book (and other Odd Mob books)!

Grammatical Agreement

Grammatical agreement: Singular and plural

The Soapbox Derby

1 Getting ready to rumble

Mr Sumo has challenged the Odd Mob to a Soapbox Derby race.

No one's more singular than Mr Sumo.

Mr Sumo **is** building a soapbox cart. Max, Flash, Googal, HMD, Wozza, Ulf and Deej **are** doing the same. They **are** all entering the Soapbox Derby but no one **is** sure who will win the race – not even Flash.

Cheesy Chad says ...

A **subject** is the person or thing that is carrying out the verb, e.g. **Ulf** is making a soapbox cart.

Singular means one, e.g. Mr Sumo. Plural means more than one, e.g. Googal and Max.

Subjects and **verbs** must agree with each other in **number**. This means that **singular subjects** go with **singular verbs** and **plural subjects** go with **plural verbs**:

<u>Shagpile</u> **is** looking forward to the race.

<u>Googal</u> and <u>Max</u> **are** looking forward to the race.

② It's the cart that's too small

Grammatical agreement: Making sense

Mr Sumo tries to squeeze himself into his cart.

Do you think my bottom looks big in this cart?
Your bottom looks big in anything!

In most cases, if the **subject** is in the **third person** (she, he or it), just add an '**s**' to a **regular verb** to make it agree:

Flash (**she**) look**s** athletic. Deej (**he**) look**s** cool. Max's hair (**it**) look**s** daft.

Top Tip: Always read through your work to see if the verb looks and sounds right with the person:

Mr Sumo look silly. ✗

Mr Sumo look**s** silly. ✓

Cheesy Chad says ...

Verbs change depending on their **person**, e.g. I speak (first person). You **speak** (second person). He, she or it **speaks** (third **person**).

Subjects and **verbs** must **agree** with each other in person:

I like to drive slowly. (First person – the speaker.)

You like to drive quickly. (Second person – the person spoken to.)

Flash likes to drive faster than a speeding bullet. (Third person – the person spoken about.)

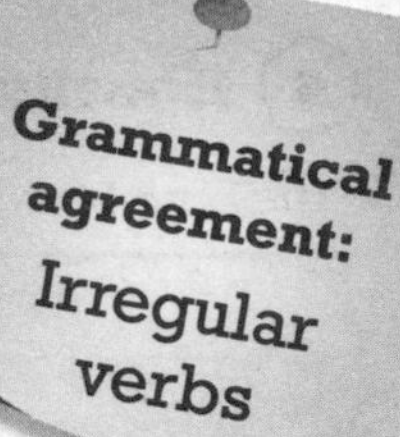

3 Back to Bedrock

Ulf hasn't quite grasped why soapbox carts are called soapbox carts.

The **others have** made their soapbox carts out of wood from soapboxes but **Ulf has** made his out of stone. This is probably not the best idea **he has** ever had but we'll find out when **they have** put the carts to the test.

Cheesy Chad says ...

Irregular verbs are little rebels. They don't follow the rules when it comes to agreeing with their subjects. You just have to memorise how they work – sorry!

The irregular verb '**to have**' becomes '**has**' when the subject is **he**, **she** or **it** (the third person):

I have heard about the Soapbox Derby. (First person)

You have heard about the Soapbox Derby. (Second person)

He has heard about the Soapbox Derby. (Third person)

Grammatical agreement:
The most irregular verb

4 Downhill racers

The Odd Mob can't believe their eyes when they see Ulf's cart.

I am astonished.
She is astonished.
We are all astonished!

There's no doubt about it -- the Odd Mob are flabbergasted!

Cheesy Chad says ...

The verb **to be** is also the **only** verb with more than one form in the past tense:
I, he, she, it **was**
You, we, they **were**

The verb **to be** is the most irregular verb in the English language:

I **am** entering the race.

You (we, they) **are** entering the race.

She (he, it) **is** entering the race.

An uphill struggle

If that cart rolls backwards, Ulf will be squashed flatter than a pancake!

Grammatical agreement: Add 'ies'

Ulf tries to pull his rock-heavy cart up to the starting line at the top of the hill while **Shagpile tries** to lend a paw – or should that be a jaw?

I'll try to push my cart up the hill.
I'll try to help.
Nothing runs faster than me.
Crikey. That Nothing must be really quick.

In the present tense, if a **verb** ends in 'y' and **he**, **she** or **it** is doing the action you can change the 'y' to 'ies' to make the **verb** agree with the **subject**:

Ulf cries with frustration when his cart won't go.

Grammatical agreement:
Add 'es'

6 What a 'to do'

Ulf has a weighty problem.

Hey,
have you just
invented the
wheel?

No, it's a
giant polo mint.

If **Ulf's cart goes** much slower he'll be in reverse. **He** really **does** need a bit of a push to get moving.

In the present tense add 'es' to the irregular verbs '**to go**' and '**to do**' if you're using the third person (he, she, it) to make them **agree** with the **subject**:

His cart does look a bit heavy but the other carts **do** look sleek.

He goes nowhere while the rest **go** racing off.

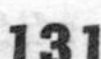

A rolling stone gathers no Ulf

Grammatical agreement: Find the subject

Somehow, Ulf persuades Shagpile to take his place in the cart.

Ulf, who has been left miles behind in the race, **has** an idea. **He**, desperate to win the Soapbox Derby, **swaps** places with Shagpile and shoves the cart over the edge of the hill.

The stone **cart**, with its canine driver, **hurtles** headlong down the hill. The only **problem**, which Ulf forgot to mention, **is** that there aren't any brakes!

Cheesy Chad says ...

A subject has to agree with the verb but if there are lots of words between the subject and the verb it's not always easy to figure out which word is the subject: The only **thought** in Shagpile's mind **was** Aghhhh!

Remember, in the present tense, if a **subject** is 'he', 'she' or 'it' the **verb** agreeing with it will end in '**s**', '**es**' or '**ies**'. Use this rule to help you spot which **verb** belongs with which **subject**:

Shagpile, who is a faithful dog, **helps** Ulf.

She, with great effort, **pushes** the soapbox cart up the hill.

The cart, completely out of control, **flies** down the hill.

8 Collision course

Watch out, Shagpile – there's trouble ahead!

Grammatical agreement:
Subjects joined by 'and'

Shagpile **and** the cart **are** in big trouble. If they don't crash into something soft, both the dog **and** the vehicle **are** doomed! Two large objects – a tree **and** Mr Sumo – **are** right in front of them. Which one will they hit?

Joke Break

Lou: How do you cure fleas on a dog?

Stu: It depends what's wrong with them.

If the two **subjects** are joined by '**and**' the **verb** will nearly always be **plural**:

Googal **and** Max **see** that disaster is about to strike. ✓
(**See** is a plural verb)

Googal **and** Max **sees** that disaster is about to strike. ✗
(**Sees** is a singular verb)

9) Happy landings

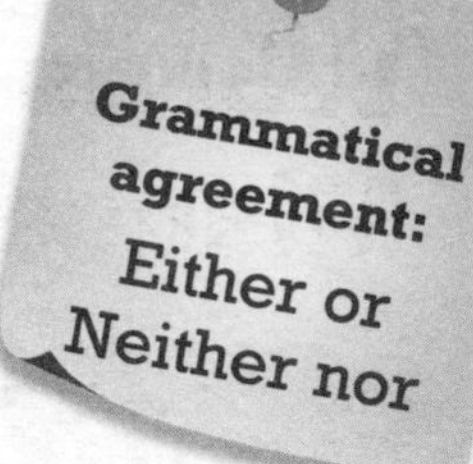

The gang can't bear to look …

Neither the gang **nor** Mr Sumo **wants** to look at what is about to happen next. **Either** he **or** the tree **is** going to be flattened – but what will become of Shagpile?

Shagpile bails out of the cart at the last moment and finds a soft place to land – though **neither** Mr Sumo **nor** the soapbox cart **looks** too happy with the outcome!

Multiple Joyce

Which of these joins two subjects?

A glue
B sticky tape
C and
D paste

If the **subjects** are joined by '**neither**' '**nor**' '**either**' or '**or**', the **verb** agrees with the subject nearest to it:

Neither the Odd Mob nor **Ulf is** bothered about the cart being smashed.

Race result – Odd Mob one, Mr Sumo lost.

Words Often Misused

Word to watch:
Lend

Take Art

1 Lend me your ears

The gang enter a kids' art contest at the local art gallery. The subject of the artwork is 'space'.

Are you entering the contest, Deej?
Yeah, everyone is. How much does it cost?
It's £3 each.
Oh no – I'm broke. Can I lend £3 please, HMD?
That's not right. You mean, 'Can I **borrow** £3?'
But I just told you – I'm broke!

Don't say **lend** when you mean **borrow**.

A person with money **lends**. A person without money **borrows**.

'May I borrow £3?' ✓ 'May I lend £3?' ✗

'Can you lend me some money?' ✓

2 Medium rare

Word to watch: Media

Max and Googal try to decide whether to do a drawing, painting or collage for the art contest.

My favourite art media is fuzzy felt. But I like clay too.
Clay is a **medium**, Max, because it's singular. So is fuzzy felt. **Media** is plural – there are several art media on this table.

Media is the **plural** of medium: one medium, two media.

Joke Break

Lou: Hear about the boy who had a green sister?

Stu: Yeah – his teacher had told him to paint his family …

Use the word **medium** for one art material:
Pencil **is** a drawing **medium**.
Use the word **media** for more than one:
Oils and watercolours **are** painting **media**.

3 Space place

Word to watch: Suppose

Ulf has been working all day on his junk model entry for the show at the art gallery.

Hey, Ulf, that's a good car park model, but you were **suppose** to do something about space.
Grhhw! I have – there's an empty space next to this BMW. So I did what I was **supposed** to.

Mmm ... who is right here? One thing is for sure – Ulf's English is better than Flash's.

I was **suppose** to do it. ✗

I was **supposed** to do it ✓

4) More or less?

Wozza finishes her painting of an alien just as Googal comes to see it.

Word to watch:
Less

Mmm, do you think I should have given it less arms?
No, I think **fewer** legs and **less** hair.

'Less arms' doesn't make sense. People often use **less** when they mean **fewer**.

Moaner Lisa

Less is used for **amounts** and fewer is used for **numbers**:

Less water ✓	Fewer people ✓
Less chance ✓	Fewer ideas ✓
Less games ✗	Fewer money ✗

5 There's only one Ulf

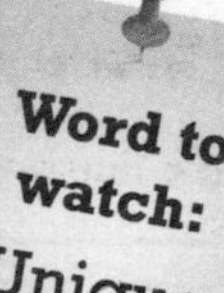
Word to
watch:
Unique

It is decision day at the art gallery. The judge is looking at the Odd Mob's entries.

Well, these entries are certainly, er, interesting. This space monster is quite unique.
Oi!
Groan ... something is either unique or not – it can't be 'quite unique'.

Googal is right. Unique means 'there's only one'. Things can't be *quite* unique or *very* unique.

Special is probably a better word most of the time.

Cheesy Chad says ...

Ulf most certainly is unique!

If something is **unique** it's the **only one** of its kind.

Word to watch: Won

6 Won nil!

Who's come first in the art contest? Let's see …

First prize goes to this superb space monster sculpture! And Mr Sumo gets the booby prize as he is too old to enter.
Hey, Ulf did it! What a brilliant idea to enter himself!
Well, none of the rest of us got an award but at least we **won** Mr Sumo.
You mean we **beat** Mr Sumo – he's not a prize. (Thank goodness!)

Don't use **won** when you mean **beat**.

Multiple Joyce

Which of these phrases makes sense?

A Fewer media
B Less unique
C Suppose to lend
D Medium wheelborrow

You can **beat** a person or team in a contest but not **win** them.
We beat City 2-0. ✓ We won City 2-0. ✗

Index

Multiple Joyce answers

page 11 Nouns – C
page 19 Plurals – C
page 29 Pronouns – D
page 35 Verbs – D
page 40 Tenses – C
page 46 Adjectives – C
page 51 Adverbs – B
page 59 Prepositions – D
page 67 Conjunctions – A
page 74 Exclamations – B
page 85 Sentences – A
page 90 Phrases – C
page 96 Clauses – D
page 101 Paragraphs – B
page 106 Word order – A
page 113 Words often confused – C
page 120 Common mistakes – A
page 125 Standard English – B
page 134 Grammatical agreement – C
page 140 Words often misused – A